TAO TE CHING

room to b
r
e
a
t
h
e

& relax

& become whole

"Dr. Condron's poetic interpretation is a beautiful work of the soul. This book has given me a way to see the beauty of receptive energy and has opened my heart and mind to the peace and stillness of Universal Truth."
- Erika Scholz, graduate student and teacher of English as a Second Language

"As I experienced this book I felt an opening sensation from my heart area. I have begun to look at my world differently. I am noticing how everyone and everything is connected and how the receptive quality and aggressive quality works together hand in hand. After each passage I am filled with a stillness in my mind, heart, body, and soul."
-Laurie Biswell, 31-year-old college student, sales associate

"The powerful images in both the Tao and the interpretation penetrate my consciousness in the most subtle and beautiful ways. This book gives me room to breathe and relax and become whole."
- Christine Madar, 35, full time volunteer

"The experience that I have with hearing the Tao is one of resonance. I can almost imagine myself as being the boarder guard asking Lao Tzu to teach me. It invokes in me a feeling that is mysterious and stirs a longing in me for the peace that it can lead to. In joy you shall depart, in peace you shall return. The Tao is my way home to peace."
- John Harrison, 46-year-old computer programmer and instructor

"The writing is like a heavenly poem that draws me into a still lake and I see what is within my soul."
-Tad Messenger, 55-year-old SOM teacher and student with a Masters degree in geology

"Learning about the Tao has birthed new awarenesses in me. I have a greater understanding of the power of receptivity. I am receiving enlightenment more as well as aggressively moving towards the ideal."
- Dave Rosemann, 24-year-old music promoter

"The statements of truth are clear, direct and refreshing. Hearing this book read out loud feels like a cool dip in a clear lake. It is soul-nourishing and peaceful, centering and enriching."
-Laurel Clark, 46-year-old teacher, minister, counselor

"I have read many translations and commentaries on the Tao Te King and never has it been so clear, simple, and transformative as these written by Dr. Condron."
- Dr. Pamela Blosser, President, School of Metaphysics

"From my experience, this book and its interpretation is highly remarkable. It is like a sweet fragrance that moves the spirit within. It truly presents the way to understand, apply, and live the essence of the receptive and aggressive principles of creation."
- Gregory Brown, 29-year-old teacher, former loan originator

*It seems as if Lao Tzu himself
has returned to give us all*

the rest of the story!

The Tao Te Ching

interpreted and explained

T^{The}AO TE CHING

interpreted and explained

A Superconscious and Subconscious Explanation
according to
Universal Principles
Universal Laws
Universal Truths
and
the Universal Language of Mind

by Dr. Daniel R. Condron

ISBN: 0-944386-30-x
Library of Congress Control Number 2003113187

Cataloging in Publication

If you desire to learn more about the research and
teachings in this book, write to School of Metaphysics
World Headquarters, Windyville, Missouri 65783.
Or call us at 417-345-8411.
Visit us on the Internet at www.som.org
& www.peacedome.org

Cover Art by Chris Sheehan Design by Shawn Campbell Frontpieces by Adam Campbell.

I would like to thank Shawn Stoner for her encouragement to complete this book and for her help in preparing the manuscript. Special thanks to my wife Barbara for the final preparation of the manuscript and for her help in the design of this book.–DRC

Foreword

I recently shared with a student that I was helping to enter into the computer the book you now hold in your hands, Dr. Daniel Condron's interpretation and explanation of the Tao Te Ching. She replied by saying, "You know, I have seen that book many times in my life, and have tried to read it, but I never understood it. It always seemed like I should understand it, and that there was really important things in it, but I never got it."

This seems to be a common response to the Tao Te Ching. There is a feeling or thought or intuitive connection to the wisdom given in this ancient Holy Work however the means to understand what it is saying, much less to apply it to the Self so that its wisdom can be used for greater spiritual growth and understanding, is most often missing.

To truly understand the Tao Te Ching requires several factors. Fortunately, these factors are mental skills that Dr. Dan (as he is called by his students) has practiced, applied and taught throughout this lifetime through his years of service in the School of Metaphysics. Combine these practices with the understandings that he brought into this lifetime from those previous, and he is perfectly situated to explain the Tao to the modern reader.

The first of these factors needed for understanding the Tao is that of stillness. Can you imagine what it means to have a still mind? To be able to cause your mind to be focused on one thing, be it a person, conversation, or project and to have it stay on that one thing *only* for as long as you desire? Can you imagine what it would be like to have a conversation and to not be thinking about what you are going to say next? Rather to be giving your full and complete attention to the person that you are in the conversation with (with no thoughts of, "What am I going to have for dinner...my, he has pretty eyes...I wonder what my boss meant by that email today?"....etc, etc.) Can you imagine what it would be like to be able to meditate and to keep your mind perfectly still, completely open to receive the wisdom of your Higher Self, your Creator?

It is this command of the attention that Dr. Dan refers to many times throughout this book as a necessity for understanding

Self and all of Creation. Many people do not believe that this type of control can be developed, they think that you either have it or you do not. However, this is not true. Anyone can be taught how to concentrate. It requires daily discipline, a strong desire, and commitment.

The importance of a still mind cannot be stressed enough for anyone who is wanting to grow spiritually. The still mind gives you objectivity in all situations, allowing you to receive a situation into your life with complete equanimity free from the pull of memory and imagination. It allows you to be fully present. There is within the common thinking, the awareness that being fully present, living in the now, is valuable and important. The understanding of how to cause this, in a step-by-step and scientific way, is what Dr. Dan and other teachers within the School of Metaphysics have been teaching for the last 30 years. Having a still mind allows you to experience all the richness of each experience in your life and through that gain all the learning that is available.

This stillness of Mind is one of the first things I noticed about Dr. Dan when I first met him. I remember thinking that there was something different about him, something strong and undefinable. At the time I didn't know what it was, but I knew that it was intriguing. Having grown up in our sensory engrossed world, I had learned, as most all of us do, that having scattered attention (multi-tasking) was a good and valuable thing. My attention had been divided from an early age by the influence of T.V., video games, and public schooling.

In Dr. Dan, I perceived something else, something new and powerful.

Eventually, through my own studies and after having more of my own experiences of stillness, I could identify what it was about Dr. Dan that was different than most. It was, and is, his capacity for stillness - "A silence that is deafening." This kind of silence is strong, powerful; it washes over you like a tidal wave that leaves behind it only the truth of what is. It reduces anything to its core essence. It eliminates confusion and scattered emotions. It allows the truth to shine through. It is this stillness.

It is this stillness of Mind that allows Dr. Dan to understand the *Tao* in the way that he does and to communicate this understanding to you. It is only in stillness that the Truth, the *Tao*, can be received and understood.

The still mind must be employed to engage the next factor required to understand the Tao Te Ching; thinking in pictures. The Mind communicates in pictures. Try this thought experiment. If you and every person you knew lost the ability to speak, however gained the ability to communicate mind to mind (telepathy), how would you communicate? Would it be in words? No. You would transmit pictures from your mind to whoever's mind you wanted to communicate with. If you wanted to say, "I need to go let my dog inside from the backyard," you would transmit an image of yourself walking to your backdoor and letting your dog in from the outside.

The truth is that all communication takes place through the transmitting of images. You have an image in your mind. Again, to use the example of letting your dog in, you say, "I need to go let my dog inside from the backyard." Your friend receives your words, and based on how well they know you, your house, and your dog, they create in their mind a picture of you walking to your backdoor and letting your dog inside. Whether this image is accurate or not depends entirely upon the accuracy of the image that they create in their mind. In other words, the more detailed and accurate the image, the more complete the communication.

The previous example seems pretty innocuous, after all, how important is it that your friend receive accurately the image of you letting your dog inside? However, the importance of complete communication becomes very apparent when we begin to consider conversations that revolve around more important topics in our lives. When you say to someone, "I love you," you obviously want them to receive the meaning that you intend.

The most important key to gaining the ability to communicate accurately is the exercising of a still mind. A still mind allows you to receive not only the words, but the thought images of the person with whom you are communicating.

All Holy Works of the world, including the Tao Te Ching, are written in this picture language, the language that we in the School of Metaphysics call the Universal Language of Mind. It is the language of our dreams, it is the language of our souls. Understanding this language is key to understanding the great teachings of all enlightened beings, because these enlightened beings understood that to communicate with the Thinker within each person, you must reach that person on a deeper level than the level of the conscious mind, physical thinking brain. This is why they taught by creating stories, parables, and poetry. All of these activate the Mind by causing there to be pictures created in the Mind of the individual, thereby speaking the language of the soul, the Universal Language of Mind.

Dr. Dan's masterful explanation of the Tao Te Ching will be beneficial and meaningful to anyone reading it. It will be of most benefit if you read it the way he wrote it, with a still mind and complete attention, thereby receiving the images that Lao Tzu created.

Read this book with a still mind and an open heart. Read each word as if it were the only word in the entire Universe. Allow the words to create pictures in your Mind and still your attention on these pictures. Let these images move into your being, cleansing your soul of anything that is keeping you away from the LIGHT.

Breath into your Self the high Truth that Dr. Dan is relating in these pages.

Let his understanding of silence and universal truth and love wash over you, so that you may perceive the glory of your own truest self.

I have had the profound privilege to have Dr. Daniel Condron as my teacher for the last 2 and 1/2 years, and I know from my own experience the power of his understanding and how it causes transformation of consciousness when one receives it and applies it. You hold in your hands the product of his understanding. Use it well.

–Shawn Stoner
August 2003, Chicago

I was observing Dr. Daniel Condron teaching his students. He was demonstrating a type of breathing to his students. As he did I observed his kundalini energy rise up his spine. It resembled heat vapors rising up his spine.

The energy then traveled to his crown chakra. Then the energy traveled to his brow chakra and out of his mouth. The image that came to my mind as I was observing was the Dragon in the *Book of Revelation* in the Bible. I wondered at the time if this was the breath of Fire.

It was so profound.

– Dr. Sheila Benjamin

And there appeared another sign in heaven;
and behold, there was a great fiery Dragon,
having seven heads and ten horns,
and seven crowns upon his heads.
–Revelation 12:3

In 516 B. C. the Keeper of the Royal Archives, which were in Wangcheng, received
a visitor from the state of Lu. The visitor
was a young man named K'ung Fu-tzu or
Confucius. Confucius was interested in
ritual and asked Lao-tzu about the ceremonies of the ancient kings.

　　Lao-tzu responded with this advice:
"The ancients you admire have been in the
ground a long time. Their bones have turned to
dust. Only their words remain. Those among
them who were wise rode in carriages when
times where good and slipped quietly away
when times were bad. I have heard that the
clever merchant hides his wealth so his store
looks empty and that the superior man acts dumb
so he can avoid calling attention to himself. I
advise you to get rid of your excessive pride and
ambition. They won't do you any good. This is
all I have to say to you."

　　Afterwards, Confucius told his
disciples, *"Today when I met Lao'tzu, it was*
like meeting a Dragon."

Introduction

For over 2000 years scholars and teachers have been trying to understand the mystery and meaning of the Tao Te Ching. Perhaps the greatest area of mystery or difficulty in understanding is the concept of non-action. The idea of non-action is referred to many times in the Tao Te Ching. Non-action is also discussed in depth in the Bhagavad Gita by Krishna.

The reason this concept has lead to confusion or difficulty for thousands of years is that most people associate non-action with passivity or even the unconsciousness of sleep.

If action is activity, work, or effort then non-action would seem to be the stoppage of effort toward one's goals. Most people do not want to stop working towards their goals or physical desires. Therefore, the concept of non-action seems unpleasant, disturbing, or distasteful and certainly not something one could strive for.

There is, however, a meaning that I have been able to discern that explains all the discrepancies and makes non-action look and seem very attractive.

Most, if not all of these difficulties fall away with the realization that expectant non-action equals receptivity. Receptivity is expectant non-action.

What are the two principles from which all creation evolves? These two great principles of creation held in Superconscious Mind are:

1. The Aggressive Principle - Yang

2. The Receptive Principle - Yin

To be aggressive is to initiate activity. To be receptive is to receive.

To be receptive is to receive the results and the benefits of one's actions and efforts to achieve, to succeed, to create, and to know the Truths of Creation. To be receptive is to be open to receive.

To be aggressive is to move forward in life, to initiate action, activity, and motion on goals, ideals and desires.

Most people want to receive. Most want to receive the good things in life. Some people confuse taking with receiving. To take is to reach out and grab something whether or not the person wants to give.

To receive is to be willing to be open to the goodness and riches of the Universe. To take is limited to one time and place. To receive is unlimited by time and space.

Receptivity has a drawing power. The power of receptivity is not only in being open and receiving but also in the capability of drawing what is needed to the Self.

The power in the aggressive quality is in moving to or toward what is needed. The power in the receptive quality is in drawing to the Self what is needed. This is seen throughout nature in the way the female-receptive attracts the male-aggressive.

In each individual there needs to be a building up and full integration of both the aggressive and receptive factors into the Self. This then leads to one becoming a whole functioning Self with a balance of aggressive and receptive within.

The enlightened masters throughout history seem to have had this capability of choosing to be either aggressive or receptive. To be yielding and soft or determined and strong as is described in the Tao Te Ching.

It seems with enlightenment comes a greater receptivity, a greater tenderness, a greater love, yet also a greater courage, commitment, fortitude, and wisdom.

Therefore, in reading this book when non-action appears in a chapter create the image in the mind's eye of receptivity, receiving and the drawing power. Then the seeming paradoxes, uncertainties, and difficulties will begin to be reduced, evaporate and disappear in the LIGHT of a greater awareness.

In order to understand the Tao or Way it is important to understand the basic structure of Mind.

The Mind consists of 3 Divisions

1. The Conscious
2. The Subconscious
3. The Superconscious

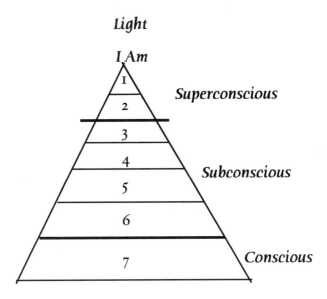

Mind is the vehicle I AM or the individual uses as a place or field of experience. Mind is the vehicle of learning for I AM. The Division of Mind called the Conscious Mind can be associated with the physical universe. Our individual conscious mind uses the 5 senses to experience in our physical universe. Our nighttime, sleeping, dreaming mind uses the subconscious mind. In the Universal Subconscious Mind we are all as souls connected. It is through this connectedness that we experience a higher perception or intuitive abilities.

Dreams come from ones individual subconscious mind which is sometimes referred to as soul. The soul or individual subconscious mind resides in the Universal Subconscious Mind. The soul or individual subconscious mind gives night dreams to the conscious mind for the purpose of the growth and learning and evolvement of the whole Self.

The Superconscious Mind holds the Divine or Perfect Plan for each individual to become enlightened, to know Self, and to know all of Mind and to learn to create.

The Subconscious and Conscious Minds provide the field of experience, the place to practice that Divine Plan in order to learn to be creators and become enlightened.

The Superconscious Mind also provides the Life Force that animates all of Mind. This Life Force makes possible life in our physical universe. It is the source of all energy.

The Tao or Way may be understood as these two factors of Superconscious Mind:

1. The Perfect or Ideal Plan to gain enlightenment
2. The Life Force to achieve the Plan of enlightenment

Thus, when Lao Tzu says in the Tao Te Ching that some particular kind of thought or action is not the Way of the Tao this may be understood as not in alignment with the Divine Plan of Creation held in Superconscious Mind. This misalignment or lack of alignment or non-attunement to Superconscious Mind leads to the person having less and less life force or energy for the physical body one is incarned into. This then leads to the soul choosing to withdraw attention from the physical body which is commonly called death.

The solution then to a long life is to be one with the Tao or Way. To be one with the Tao is to align ones conscious mind to ones soul purpose or subconscious mind and attune both to Superconscious Mind which is the High Self. This attunement gives one the life force, energy, enlightenment and wherewithal to bring planet Earth and its inhabitants to greater enlightenment. This is the Way of the Tao.

The word Tao means Way or Road. The Way includes everything in the universe or the whole Mind. The Tao is the way to harmonize with and come to know the whole Mind and thereby the whole Self.

The word Te means power, integrity, or virtue. Te is the individual Self, inner soul Self, or the individual mind.

The world Ching means scripture or classic. Ching was in ancient times of China the thread used to hold beads together. In this way the word ching is akin to the word sutra from which the word sutra derives which means to bind or tie together. The word sutra is used in the book, The Yoga Sutras of Patanjali, which is a classic of Indian sacred or Holy literature. I interpreted and explained the Yogi Sutras of Patanjali over a decade ago in a book I wrote and titled, Dreams of the Soul.

Therefore, the Tao Te Ching may be interpreted as,

The Way the Self follows to unite the conscious, subconscious, and superconscious minds, or

the Way the Individual may develop the power to become enlightened scripture, or

the Way of connectedness between the conscious mind and the superconscious mind, or

the Way to connect the individual conscious mind to all of Mind and I AM.

I have found that interpreting and explaining the Yogi Sutras of Patanjali has well prepared me for interpreting and explaining the Tao Te Ching. As did my efforts in interpreting and explaining the *Book of Matthew* from the Bible titled: The Universal Language of Mind, the Book of Matthew Interpreted.

As much as I am fulfilled in explaining the inner and Superconscious meaning of the Tao Te Ching, in some ways I am more thrilled from this interpretation of Holy Scripture. In each chapter, I strived to merge my mind with the Tao. At times it seemed my mind merged with the thoughts or consciousness of Lao Tzu.

I experience a sense of gladness and fulfillment in being able to offer the Tao Te Ching to the world in a form that is understandable to anyone desiring to know the Truth of Self, Mind, and Creation.

The Universal Language of Mind is the language of pictures. Words are abstract concepts that convey an idea or picture. When you read the word blue you may picture or image the color blue. Upon hearing the word blue you may picture or image the color blue. Upon hearing the word tree one may picture a maple tree, a pine tree, or a poplar tree.

To speak a sentence or have a conversation one holds a picture in mind and then uses words to describe the picture.

We think in pictures or images rather than words or phrases. The enlightened people that wrote the Holy Books of the world knew and understood this. They therefore, wrote in ways that convey powerful images in the mind of the reader. They also recognized that as people become more evolved their perception increases. Therefore, the ability to understand Holy Scriptures on a deeper level is available.

The authors of these Holy Books wrote in such a way as to aid anyone reading a Holy Book to reach deeper within the Self for greater understanding of the meaning, purpose, and process of creation and life.

When words are read or spoken the mind converts those words, sentences, paragraphs or phrases into mind pictures or mental images. When a person speaks or writes it is like a movie projector or video play showing movies in the minds of others.

The enlightened beings who wrote the Holy Scriptures of the World knew the Universal Language of Mind is pictures. Sometimes they focused on Universal Truths. Always they expressed the universals that each individual needs to understand in order to become and be enlightened. I have applied the Universal Language of Mind to understanding and explaining the Tao Te Ching and in addition I have utilized the Universal Truths, Universal Laws and Universal Principles. All may be best understood from the standpoint of receptivity and a still mind.

The Universal Language of Mind is the language that your subconscious mind uses to communicate to you each night when you go to sleep in the form of dreams. At night we dream. The conscious mind and brain receive the dream from ones subconscious mind. The dream is a mental image or picture. Then it is up to the dreamer to apply, use, and integrate the knowledge received into the conscious mind and then the whole Self. Learning begins by receiving. Each night we receive a dream whether we remember it or not. Remembering dreams is a skill that can be taught. I have taught thousands to do so.

Just as learning from night dreams begins by receiving the dream and recording it in a dream notebook, so a baby also learns by receiving. When a baby is born the child receives nourishment, comfort, love, security, shelter and clothing. In return the infant grows very rapidly, mentally, and physically. The baby then practices what is received. We call it play. The infant then learns to talk and walk.

So you see all learning and growth is dependent upon receiving. What is received mentally is images or moving, mental pictures. The Chinese at the time of the writing of the Tao Te Ching wrote in pictograms or pictures rather than writing with an alphabet. They still write in this form in the present.

The Tao Te Ching is sometimes referred to as mysterious. My perspective is that anything can be understood. It can be productive to read the Tao Te Ching and try to make sense of it or to try to imagine what it might be saying. I believe it is much more valuable and productive to understand anything one reads, to be able to receive the mental image or picture the author is conveying with words.

The Tao Te Ching was not originally written with an alphabet. It was written with pictograms which are basically pictures. Before the invention of the alphabet supposedly by the ancient Phoenicians everyone around the world wrote in pictures. Sometimes these pictures are called pictograms or pictoglyphs or hieroglyphics.

The ancient Egyptians wrote in the picture language. They used hieroglyphics. The Aztecs at the time of Cortez the Spanish conquistador wrote books in pictograms. The Mayans had a vast amount of books written in the picture language. It wasn't until the latter part of the 20th century that the Mayan written language began to be deciphered.

The point is, many if not all of these ancient peoples wrote in pictures and did not have an alphabet. An alphabet, while promoting efficiency and accuracy in conveying messages, is abstract and far removed from the actual mental image being conveyed.

The Chinese never made the shift from writing in pictures to using an alphabet. Although in the present time period Chinese written characters do not seem to resemble the idea or image presented, originally the picture or pictograph looked more like the object or subject. The symbol for the Tao or Way is π. This symbol π is a gateway. It is the gateway through which we are constantly passing for the Way or Tao is everywhere. A gateway is a way to pass from one place to another. This is exactly what our consciousness does.

The Chinese graphs or pictographs or picture writing for the Tao Te Ching at the time of the writing were:

1. a head, moon, or eye looking straight ahead
2. a heart
3. a sign for movement

Putting these three components together we have:

1. vision, perception, goal or ideal symbolized by the eye looking straight ahead

2. permanent and lasting understanding and love symbolized by the heart

3. action, effort, or energy given forth symbolized by movement

Putting this all together we have perception or ideal that one is fully committed to, with a purpose of fully understanding the lessons of life, combined with activity, action, effort, or movement needed to make it so.

These three factors of ideal or goal-imagination-eye, and purpose-understanding-heart, and activity or effort-movement are necessary for any success be it mental, emotional or physical.

Ideal, purpose and activity are the three factors needed for success, especially mental and spiritual success.

Ideal is the image of who and what you want to become.

Purpose is personal benefit and the greatest benefit is to become enlightened.

Activity is the expenditure of energy needed to achieve ones inner urge and need.

In order to apply the mind most successfully to an ideal, purpose and activity one must apply the aggressive and receptive universal principles.

From Chinese philosophy, history and science we have two words to describe the Aggressive and Receptive Principles. Those two words are Yin and Yang.

Yang is the Aggressive Principle
Yin is the Receptive Principle

Sometimes people confuse the words aggressive and aggression. To be aggressive is to direct the mind and initiate action or effort towards one's goals and ideals. To practice aggression is to use force to try to control someone or something.

Just as the words aggressive and aggression have different meaning so also do receptive and passive have different meanings.

To be receptive is to still the mind and use the will to draw to the Self the learning, people, and experiences needed for learning and growth.

In order to understand the Tao Te Ching one must understand these basic principles for they are the basis upon which the Tao is written. The Tao Te Ching's focus is on the power of the receptive quality. I did not learn about or come to understand the aggressive and receptive principles in the major university I attended. Rather through intense study of Self and Mind these Universal Principles became apparent.

I have applied the Universal Language of Mind to the Tao Te Ching. It is the same language as given in night dreams. It is the hidden or secret language of all Holy Works. It is the language of the Yogi Sutras of Patanjali of which I have written in my book, Dreams of the Soul, the Yogi Sutras of Patanjali. It is also the language of the Bible that I used to interpret the *Book of Matthew*.

Tao is the all pervading energy of cosmic or universal unity from which all created things emanate and return.

Tao Te Ching means the Way of Power Classic

Tao Te Ching means the Road and Integrity Classic

Te signifies qualities or strengths of the individual, the Self.

Te is what you are, the individual expression of Tao.

Te is the individual soul, the individual mind.

Tao is the entire creation, the whole mind

Te is power, integrity and virtue

Ching means scripture or a classic book or scripture

The chief lesson of the Bhagavad Gita is one should act without desire for the fruits of one's actions. The fruits of one's actions are the physical results, particularly the pleasurable results that engross one in the senses or the conscious ego.

The Tao Te Ching mentions non-action many times. Another way to view non-attachment is action without attachment.

Lao Tzu was a native of Huhsien province in the state or country of Ch'u. The name Lao Tzu means old Master. Lao Tzu was a master of his mind and a master of his self, his ego and had surrendered to the will of I AM. His personal name was Erh (meaning ear and therefore learned). A name given to him later was Tan which means long-eared and therefore wise. At the time of Lao Tzu the area that was to become the country of China was not yet united. Instead the land area was divided or separated into many smaller warring states.

Lao Tzu was the head librarian and therefore, kept the archives at the Chou dynasty at the capital of Loyang which was about 300 kilometers west of Huhsien. The area of Loyang later became known as Wangcheng. In the year 516 B.C. Lao Tzu the keeper of the Royal Archives received a visitor from the neighboring state of Lu. The visitor was a young man named K'ung Fu'tzu or Confucius. It is interesting to note that both beings had the name or title "tzu" which means master.

Central China

These maps depict the area in which Lao Tzu lived. They give a picture or image of that area of Asia much different from modern China. In the time of Lao Tzu there were many separate states or feudal kingdoms existing in what is presently China. These states were often at war just as the feudal kingdoms of Europe were often at war from the Dark and Middle Ages up to the present.

It was this constant warring and mismanagement of the empires that Lao Tzu experienced and wrote about in the Tao Te Ching. He wrote the Tao Te Ching in such a way that it applied first of all to the individual yet also it applied to the state. In this way, the teachings of Lao Tzu in the Tao Te Ching are universal.

According to Ssu-ma Ch'ien, Confucius was interested in ritual and asked Lao Tzu about the ceremonies of the ancient kings. Lao

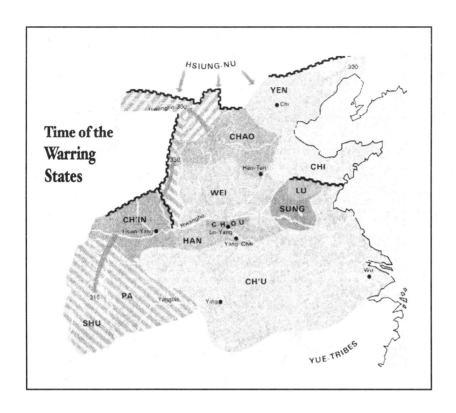

Time of the Warring States

HSIUNG-NU

YEN

Chi

CHAO

Han-Tan

CHI

WEI

LU

SUNG

CH'IN

Hsien-Yang

CH.O U

Lo-Yang

HAN

Yang-Chai

Hwangho

Hwangho 300

330

300

CH'U

Wu

PA

Yangtse

Ying

316

SHU

YUE-TRIBES

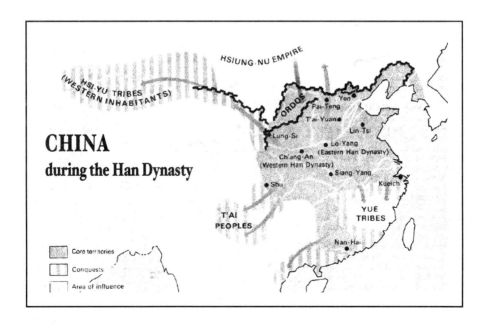

CHINA during the Han Dynasty

HSIUNG-NU EMPIRE

HSI-YU TRIBES (WESTERN INHABITANTS)

ORDOS

Yen

Pai-Teng

T'ai-Yuan

Lin-Tsi

Lung-Si

Lo-Yang (Eastern Han Dynasty)

Ch'ang-An (Western Han Dynasty)

Siang-Yang

Shu

Kueich

T'AI PEOPLES

YUE TRIBES

Nan-Hai

Core territories

Conquests

Area of influence

Tzu responded with this advice: *"The ancients you admire have been in the ground for a long time. Their bones have turned to dust. Only their words remain. Those among them who were wise rode in carriages when times were good and slipped quietly away when times were bad. I have heard that the clever merchant hides his wealth so his store looks empty and that the superior man acts dumb so he can avoid calling attention to himself. I advise you to get rid of your excessive pride and ambition. They won't do you any good. This is all I have to say to you."*

Afterwards, Confucius told his disciples, *"Today when I met Lao-Tzu, it was like meeting a dragon."*

The Dragon is a symbol for the ego. It is also a symbol for the awakened Kundalini, the creative power and energy in all of us that resides at the base of the spine. Kundalini is a word from India that means Serpent Fire.

As one becomes enlightened the sleeping Dragon, the ancient Serpent referred to in the book of Revelation, rises up the spine enlivening and vivifying the 7 major energy centers called chakras thus revealing the mysteries of higher consciousness to the individual. All enlightened masters have raised the Kundalini Dragon or Serpent as did most assuredly Lao-tzu. This is why Confucius describes his meeting with Lao-tzu as being like meeting a Dragon.

Because I have experienced the Kundalini and the chakras and the serpent and the Dragon, I read and interpret the Tao Te Ching from this perspective. It is the perspective from which it was written.

The raised Kundalini that leads to mastery of the Dragon which is enlightenment is the destiny of each individual and of all humanity. The rate at which each person causes this to happen is a function of choices, imaging, desire and will. Therefore, sooner or later we become enlightened. Lao-tzu gained enlightenment 2,500 years ago as did Gautama the Buddha, Mahavira, Pythagoras, Zarathustra and Confucius. Individuals have continued to become enlightened since that time. And individuals became enlightened before then also.

The time period of Lao Tzu and the writing of the Tao Te Ching was one of great new awareness and enlightenment for there were many great spiritual teachers who were masters that lived during this time period. The following is some information and knowledge about some of these great beings. Knowing about them helps in placing the Tao Te Ching in proper context in regard to its role and function in aiding the consciousness of developing humankind.

Confucius brought to China and the world a greater system and awareness of morality and ethics. He brought a code of living to the world. Confucius (about to 479 B.C.) is the name we call K'ung Fu Tzu which means K'ung the Master.

His real name was K'ung Ch'iu. Born in the state of Lu which is the modern Shantung Province, his entire teaching was practical and ethical rather than religious. He restored the ancient morality and taught that proper outward acts based on the five virtues of kindness, uprightness, principles, wisdom and faithfulness comprise the whole duty of the individual.

Reverence for parents, living and dead, was one of his key concepts.

In the following centuries the influence of his teachings became so great that they helped mold the Chinese nation.

He lived at a time when feudalism had degenerated in China, while crime and wars were everywhere. Confucius believed that the solution was to bring the people once more to the principles and ideals of the Sages of antiquity. While serving as minister of crime in the state of Lu at age 50, he almost completely eliminated crime.

Lao Tzu brought to the world in the Tao Te Ching, the awareness of creation and Self particularly as it relates to the receptive principle. I have found that the Tao Te Ching relates to most and probably all the world's great Holy Scriptures in one way or another. Lao Tzu brought a greater understanding of receptivity and surrender of the ego to LIGHT into the World.

The story is that Lao Tzu upon losing his position as keeper of the royal archive due to war decided to leave the country. He realized the country was degenerating and had little chance for enlightened rule. So he headed west for Hanku Pass which served as the border between the Chou dynasty and the neighboring state of China.

When Lao Tzu arrived at the pass Yin Hsi who was warden of the pass recognized the Sage and asked to be taught before Lao Tzu could pass. So Lao Tzu wrote the Tao Te Ching which is the essence of his teaching and gave it to Yin Hsi. Lao Tzu was then allowed to continue on to other lands and thus we have this wonderful book today.

Gautama the Buddha (563-483 B.C. ?) brought the under-standing and use of the Mind to humanity. He made a science and a religion of the practice and use of the Mind. He also greatly expanded the awareness and knowledge of Dharma in the world. This Dharma is explained in the Dhammapada or Dharmapada of which I quote often in this book.

Gautama the Buddha was a master teacher and founder of Buddhism. Born in Kapila Vastu, India near the border of Nepal. He was originally named Prince Siddhartha. In later life he was known as Sakyamuni which means Sage of the Sakyas.

The name Gautama the Buddha is a combination of the family name Gautama and Buddha which means enlightened one.

He realized that suffering is the common experience of humanity. He renounced possessions.

He experienced in meditation the great enlightenment which revealed the way of salvation from suffering.

He gave his first sermon at Deer Park, near Benares. He was one of the greatest of beings. His influence helped to reform Hinduism.

His great reasoning abilities introduced scientific thought in a new way to India.

His life and teachings have influenced the lives of more than half the human race.

Vardhamana Mahavira (approx. 549 B.C. to ?) brought the science and religion of non-violence to the world. It was not that he was the first to teach this, yet neither were any of these great masters the first to teach their subject. Rather they refined, reformed, and expanded upon older religions, older forms of presentation. The Jain religion came as an outgrowth of Mahavira's teachings.

Mahavira means great Hero. The founder of Jainism who denied the Divine Authority and authority of the Vedas, taught worship of spiritual beings called Jinas (conquerors) which are saviors from entrapment in physical existence and the cycle of rebirth. Jains hold these enlightened beings to be greater than the gods of the Hindu pantheon.

Mahavira taught a reverence for all life. Was the last of the 24 Tirthankaras which means fully enlightened teachers.

Mahavira taught austerity, non-violence, vegetarianism, and the acceptance of the 5 great vows of renunciation. Probably a younger contemporary of Gautama the Buddha and lived in the same general area of India.

Mahavira's father's name was Siddhartha which is interesting since Gautama the Buddha's first name was also Siddhartha.

Mahavira developed the teaching of ahimsa or nonviolence. He encouraged his followers to practice vegetarianism which has been credited with helping to bring an end to animal sacrifice in India.

Taught the 5 great vows of renunciation of killing, of speaking untruths, of greed, sexual pleasure, and all other attachments to living beings and non-living things. Mohandas K. Gandhi was raised a Jain and as such as taught the science of nonviolence as a child. From this, he became Mahatma Gandhi and freed India from British rule.

Pythagoras (582-500 B.C.), often called the Father of Numbers, brought a greater understanding of the science of numbers to the Greeks and through them to the Romans and from the Romans to what became western civilization.

Pythagoras was a Greek philosopher and mathematician born in Samos. He was the founder of the Pythagorean School, which had a lasting influence on the course of ancient science, philosophy, and theology in Greece, Alexandria Egypt, and through the Roman Empire.

Pythagoras was initiated into the inner secrets of life, Self, and mind-creation by the Egyptian priests as well and the Holy Ones of India. He settled in Crotona, a Greek colony in southern Italy where he founded his school.

Obedience, silence and Self examination were taught as a foundation for the teachings of numbers, astrology, and music. Sacred geometry was a key element taught. Pythagoras also taught immortality and reincarnation.

Pythagoras said he had a memory of all his previous existence or lifetimes. Pythagoras taught mathematics as a science and laid the foundation for all later developments in geometry in the western world.

He also taught astrology as a science and that numbers are the basis of all things.

Zarathustra (about 660 B.C.-583 B.C. ?) or Zoroaster as the Greeks called him, brought a teaching of the power or forces of LIGHT and Darkness to the world. In this way he was similar to Lao Tzu who gives much attention to Light and Darkness also.

Was a Master Teacher of ancient Persia, which is present day Iran. He is considered to be the founder of the religion known as Zoroastrianism or Zarathustraism.

As an adolescent he experienced revelation of a new religion. He began teaching the new way of thinking, the new religion at about the age of 30. His first convert was his cousin. At the age of 42 or 12 years later he converted Vishtaspa the King of Bactria in eastern Persia to the new religion.

The new faith spread quickly. Zarathustra is probably the author of the Gathas, a group of religious poems written in an archaic form of Persian. The Gathas form part of the Zend-Avesta the sacred book or scriptures of Zoroastrianism.

The religion of Zarathustra heavily influenced Judaism, Christianity, and Islam.

Each of these individuals contributed to the upliftment of consciousness on the planet Earth. All lived in the same general time period. It seems that time period was crucial in the development of the consciousness of humanity.

The Old Testament of the Bible was also being written in part during this time period. The Bible was then added to after the time of Jesus who became the Christ.

The reader is invited where a Bible passage is quoted to turn to the Bible passage and read the entire chapter for even greater perspective.

I have used and employed the Universal Language of Mind in this book often to give insight and to make a passage more understandable to the reader. I have also employed the Universal Laws and Universal Truths in the explanations in order that the reader may understand the Mind, the Tao, and all of Creation.

The Bible passages quoted help to unite East and West Holy Works or teachings in a way that the reader may find easy to understand or at least intrigue the reader to look deeper. The key to remember is that these teachings are Universal whether in the Bible or the Tao Te Ching or the Dharmapada or the Bhagavad Gita. The

Universal Truths are timeless and have always been available on planet Earth.

The Tao Te Ching presents the subject of nature often. The importance of being in harmony with nature is emphasized. I grew up on a farm in northwest Missouri. It is a family farm that has been in the Condron family for five generations.

The farm has a woods or timber as our family called it. It was there in the timber that I played many hours and days as I was growing up.

I noticed that when I sat down next to a large tree, such as a big, giant, white oak tree that I drew energy from that tree. I would sit down with my back to the tree and would actually feel the energy pouring into my back and then through my body. That large oak tree was giving energy and consciousness to me. In addition, Mother Earth was giving to me through that tree.

I never felt alone in those wooded hills. I experienced my connectedness with the trees, the plants and all of nature.

The Earth and trees healed me. Mother Earth nurtured me. I can remember as a young boy drawing strength, healing, and energy from the trees in the timber.

I noticed that when I ran on the grass of a pasture, I could run a long way without getting winded, but when I tried to run on dirt, cinders, or gravel I soon became winded and out of breath.

The farm I grew up on is divided up into 40 acre sections which measure 1/4 of a mile on each side. My great, great Grandfather planted rows of hedge trees, also known as Bodarc, the full quarter mile length forming natural tree fences of thorny underbrush.

By the time I was growing up in the 1960's, the trees were fully grown, being over 80 years old. The lower limbs had fallen off forming a quarter mile long canopied tunnel. The large graceful limbs came out from the tree at 10 foot high and more and then after stretching out 10 to 20 feet drooped to the ground. This formed a wonderful natural tunnel, that a young boy could run through.

I noticed as I ran through this tunnel starting on the north and running south that it seemed like I could run forever. I would run and run occasionally dodging a small bush. I could feel the natural energy surrounding me. I received that energy into myself and loved the experience. I enjoyed the freedom of infinite or inexhaustible energy as the Tao Te Ching calls it.

I grew up, went to college and became involved in learning in cities. After many years I moved to a rural, country setting once again. Then I began to understand on a higher level all the energy, all that I had received from nature as a young boy. I remember after I had returned to the country and had lived there for about a year, I said to my wife Barbara, "I had forgotten what it is like to live in the country!" Now I remember and I will never forget it again.

Nature and Mother Earth are a very important part of the Tao. The Tao Te Ching's focus is aligned with Mother Earth and thus, nature. Therefore, in order to understand and know the Tao it helps to know nature and Mother Earth.

The subject of breath, prana, and life force are also presented in the Tao Te Ching. Physical breath is a way we receive prana into the physical body. Prana or life force fills the Universe and is everywhere. Few people know how to make conscious use of it for their health, well being and enlightenment.

When I was a boy I remember there were times when I couldn't take my attention off my breath. This became an annoyance to me because I wanted to give my attention to playing, running, jumping and the things children do.

Now from my years of commitment to know myself and my use of meditation, concentration, visualization, and life force-breath, I understand the value of breath. I know from experience the value of prana, life force and the vital breath. I realize I had permanent understandings of the disciplined use of breath when I chose to enter this lifetime.

The use of life breath or prana is an invaluable aid for any individual desiring to know Self. Breath is the factor that binds the soul to the physical body. The disciplined use and understanding of the vital, life breath or prana frees the Self to use the whole mind and to know the whole Self.

Therefore, anytime breath is mentioned in the Tao Te Ching, it is of great importance to use the wisdom and knowledge given. A still mind combined with breath-life force can go a long way towards aiding the individual in the quest for enlightenment.

In the present time period more and more people are "waking up" in awareness and consciousness as the mental and spiritual evolution of humanity is accelerated. Each individual's consciousness is raised by their desire and effort coupled with the efforts of those who teach them in order that they may achieve this high state of Superconscious awareness. This high state of knowing Self, Mind and Creation is also known as Buddha Consciousness, Cosmic Consciousness or Christ Consciousness.

When the Kundalini Serpent or Dragon is raised from the base of the spine and then rises up the spine and out through the crown of the head the individual experiences the Tao, eternity, the Mother principle, and the inexhaustible source of everything.

This interpretation and explanation of the Tao Te Ching was written to aid any individual, any person, who desires to know the Self and purpose of life and creation to quicken that awareness and understanding.

Planet Earth or Mother Earth is evolving even as the souls inhabiting Earth are evolving. This book can aid or help in the quickening of the Way. For to understand the Way better, to have greater awareness of the Way is to open the possibility to more rapid soul growth and spiritual development as one grows in consciousness.

TAO TE CHING
interpreted and explained

A *Superconscious* and *Subconscious* Explanation
according to
Universal Principles
Universal Laws
Universal Truths
and
the Universal Language of Mind

by Dr. Daniel R. Condron

One

A Way that can be walked is not the eternal Way
A Name that can be named is not the Eternal Name

Tao is both named and nameless
The Named is the Mother of ten thousand things

For this reason,
A still mind in a thought-free state may perceive
the mind's essence and one's true and permanent
Nature
A busy mind filled with thoughts sees only
the outer forms of mind and the world

This pair of essence and manifestation are
connected at the source
They differ in what we call them
Yet this unity and oneness
is the mystery of the original principle
The doorway to the knowledge of one's true nature

One of the qualities of our physical universe is that it is tempo-rary. The physical universe is designed to be a temporary school or place of learning for the real and lasting identity that is the individual. This real identity has been known throughout the ages as I AM.

The first creation of the Creator was LIGHT. Following the First Creation came the creation of individualized units of LIGHT known as I AM or plural I AMs.

All creation begins as a thought. Before any creation takes on physical form it is first a thought. The original LIGHT of creation was formless. To name something is to separate and identify its form as separate and distinct from other forms.

In the Bible the *Book of Genesis*, chapter one verse three states, *"And God said, Let there be light; and there was light."*

Also in *Genesis 2:19, "And out of the ground the Lord God formed every beast of the field, and every fowl of the air; and brought them to Adam to see what he would call them; and whatever Adam called every living creature, that was its name."*

Before Adam named the creatures they were without iden-tification. The symbolic meaning of this in both the Tao Te Ching and the Bible is that before energy or consciousness takes on form it is formless yet in a potential state that is ready to be used and directed. To name something is to recognize its form and form is a powerful factor of physical life and the Conscious Mind.

The physical environment in which we live is the final outward manifestation of LIGHT. LIGHT is the first creation of the Creator.

The eternal Tao is eternal creation and its essence is LIGHT. The nature of spirit is eternal. The nature of the physi-cal body is temporary. One who thinks physically, one who is engrossed in the physical senses and doesn't recognize his own entrapment in a physical body, can not understand the higher nature or vibration of energy and consciousness. The eternal creation or Tao is energy and substance vibrating at a higher rate of vibration than our five physical senses can perceive. This higher vibration is meaningless to one engrossed in physical existence because in order to name something you must first perceive and identify that something.

There are over 10,000 things one can perceive and identify on our physical Earth. Therefore, you can name them which is to separate and identify them. This is productive yet when one is controlled by physical desires then the attention is held bound on physical forms and objects and things. Then one ceases to identify the learning in the use of physical objects.

The one who is using the physical existence to build permanent understandings of Self, creation, soul growth, and spiritual development understands the Subconscious and Conscious Minds. Such a one can understand the manifestations being constantly created in the life. Such a one understands thought is cause. Such a one creates only the highest desires and the desires are for soul growth and spiritual development.

Everyone has an inner urge which is the desire to be like their Creator. Children desire to be like their parents.

Everything began formless. Everything was created from the essence of Creator. Everything and everyone has deep within its being the desire to be like a creator and evolve into and en-LIGHT-ened soul.

All desires are to be used to build permanent understandings of Self and Creation. As desires are fulfilled and evolved to the need for enlightenment, soul growth is quickened. The soul fulfills spiritual needs for awareness and higher consciousness and attains a universal or unity consciousness.

The lesson is:

Discipline the mind until the still mind is achieved. Use desires for permanent learning and growth.

5

Two

Everyone can perceive beauty because other things
    seem ugly
Everyone can perceive good because other things
    seem bad or sinful.

Possessing and not possessing arise together
Difficult and easy complement each other
Long and short define each other
High and low determine each other
Silence and sound harmonize with each other
Before and after follow one another

Therefore, the thinker works by being still
and teaches by showing instead of telling
The Sage creates but does not possess
completes without dwelling on it

Creating without attachment
Action without engrossment
Activity is achieved yet attention
does not remain on the action
Therefore, he does not identify with limitations
Therefore, the full benefit of the experience lasts
forever

The original creation of LIGHT desiring to manifest form, divided or became two parts or halves known as Yin and Yang which are the Receptive and Aggressive Principles of Creation.

The aggressive quality is the initiating factor.
The receptive quality is the receiving factor.
The aggressive quality pushes forward.
The receptive quality draws to itself.

All the Universe proceeds from these two qualities. Together the aggressive and receptive creates a third. This is the three part creation known in all great religions and many Holy Books from around the world.

In the Bible this triad is known as, the Father, Son and Holy Spirit or Whole Mind. The word spirit also means or can be translated as Mind.

In the Mahabarata from India the trinity is known as Brahma, Vishnu, and Shiva. This three part creation we see around us every day. It is around us as a father and a mother creating a child. It is present in one plant pollinating another to form a seed.

The Aggressive and Receptive Principles of Creation form, create, and make possible the Superconscious Mind. The Superconscious Mind is a balance of the Aggressive and Receptive Principles of Creation. These two create a third. From these three proceed the seven levels of Mind, the seven universes. From these seven levels of Mind come twelve major aspects of Self and 144,000 opportunities to learn through the myriad of minor aspects of the Self.

Thus, the One becomes the Two. The Two becomes the Three. The Three becomes the Seven. The Seven becomes the 12 and the 12 becomes the 144,000 which are the 144,000 aspects of Self and of Creation.

The Aggressive and Receptive Principles of Creation manifest into physical existence as the pairs of opposites. While in a physical body and physical existence we are under the influence of these pairs of opposites such as hot and cold, good and bad, right and wrong, up and down, good and evil.

These opposites give us boundaries of extremes and in so doing give rise to form. Humanity is moving forward in consciousness from childlike beginnings of reasoning. Humanity needs these pairs of opposites in order to learn about the Aggressive and Receptive Principles of Creation. In a similar manner a child needs boundaries in order to be safe and to learn.

In adulthood of reasoning humanity needs to expand beyond these boundaries and therefore, the pairs of opposites. Beyond judgements of good and bad is eternal learning, growth, forward motion and expansion of consciousness. Therefore, the learned one, the one having achieved reasoning who is moving to the next stage of evolutionary growth called intuition stills the mind and instead of judging, learns from the experience.

The wise one, the thinker, the knower, the illumined one, is a creator. Such a one creates every day without becoming engrossed or entrapped in the creations. The wise one uses activity, action, work, and effort for the purpose of producing permanent understandings, permanent learning for the soul. The work may be temporary but the soul learning and spiritual development are eternal. They remain with the soul forever.

The world is filled with the pairs of opposites. One can get distracted for lifetimes. The ideal of all effort is to improve the Self, to uplift, and add to one's consciousness and to grow as a soul. Therefore, purpose is necessary in all activity in order to add rapidly to one's soul understanding. Keep the attention on the learning of Universal Laws and Truths and apply them to oneself rather than thinking about the physical activity that has already passed.

How would one know what possessing is without the experience of possessing? One needs experience in order to learn.

Teaching is showing because showing engages more of the senses than just telling someone what to do. Therefore, the opportunity for learning is greater.

The lesson is:
All experiences in physical life are temporary.
Therefore, learn, release, transform and move to the higher learning.

Three

Giving no special honors prevents people from
     scheming and competing
Not valuing hard to obtain goods prevents people
from
     stealing
Not displaying objects of desire will cause
     the people's minds to be undisturbed

Therefore, the Sage rules and leads by
stilling minds and opening hearts
filling their inner being
weakening their personal ambitions
and strengthening their character

He teaches people to be simple
     and without desires
Then the cunning and crafty will not dare to take
     advantage of them
When one practices expectant non-action
then all is ordered and in harmony with nature

3

When pride is removed and replaced with humbleness then is open and honest communication possible. When one is open to learning, then a free giving and receiving of energies is possible.

The nature of physical existence is temporary. Therefore, all physical things that are accumulated will be lost or left behind. When the attention is placed upon building permanent soul understandings the learning is made a part of Self forever. Once it is a part of Self it is yours forever.

Refusing to be lured into engrossment in the physical senses and their attendant desires for physical things helps keep the Self focused on the heart's desire which is soul growth and spiritual development.

The wise individual rules and directs all the many aspects of Self best when the heart center is full of love. This love must flow freely from the heart. Yet as it empties the love of the heart is continually replenished.

The greatest nourishment is food for the soul and food for the soul is the knowledge made a part of the Self called permanent understandings. This is called filling the inner being.

Instead of having great ambitions for physical objects and positions of power, thirst for fulfilling the inner Soul urge of enlightenment. Then you will have a firm foundation and a strong structure for building enlightenment within the Self. When attention is placed on what is really important in life which is soul growth, enlightenment, love and caring for others, the brain and its attendant habits cannot rule the mind or the Self.

The structure of Mind is simple. It is our five physical senses and the physical brain that make life complicated.

To be simple is to uncomplicate one's mind. It is to still the restless thoughts of the mind and receive the Universal Truths of Creation. Then the physical desires no longer rule the Self.

Then the brain and the five senses no longer control the Self. One who is ruled by the senses and the brain is an intellectual. One who has mastered the Mind is a wise soul, an enlightened being and is fulfilling life's purpose.

One who is mastering the mind can expand the consciousness to all of creation. A being such as this lives in a connected consciousness and teaches the Universal Laws and the Universal Truths of Mind. Thus the teaching is Universal.

The lesson is:
Learn
the universal lessons of life and apply them to
Self for mind is simple.

Four

The Tao is a limitless space
Yet its use is inexhaustible
It is like the unfathomable source
filled with infinite possibilities

It dulls the sharp edges
Unties the tangled knot
Settles the dust

So still, so calm and deep
but ever present and enduring

I do not know whose child it is
It seems to have existed before Te (the Lord)

God created the Heaven and the Earth in the very beginning. *"And the Earth was without form, and void; and darkness was upon the face of the deep. And the Spirit of God moved upon the face of the water. And God said, 'Let there be Light'; and there was Light. And God saw that the Light was good; and God separated the Light from the darkness. And God called the Light Day, and the darkness he called Night. And there was evening and there was morning. The first day." (Genesis 1:1-5)*

This limitless expansion of LIGHT creates a limitless space. The more one grows into the LIGHT of awareness and understanding the more one's sharp edges of fear, anger, doubt, guilt, resentment, hatred, and other hurts are worn down. The sharp edges of an individual lead to a sharp tongue that can hurt people and the Self. The more enlightened one is, the more enlightened one can teach with wisdom and insight.

The LIGHT of awareness untangles the twisted and unconscious memory thinking in the brain. The complicated ways of thinking that create knots of limitation in thoughts and consciousness are untied and unraveled when the thoughts in one's mind are caused to be still. Then thought can be simple and clear.

LIGHT which permeates everything in creation is the Tao. It is the child of the Creator. LIGHT was created before Te, which is the Lord which symbolizes I AM. I AM is an individualized unit of LIGHT. The eternal creation called LIGHT is the source of everything we experience in the universe and more. The eternal creation is in continual forward motion. It is unlimited. Each person can create and use creation and the energy of creation. Yet it is always there waiting for individuals to learn to be creators. Become one with this substance of Creation; for it is the abode of the Real Self.

The LIGHT is within every being. It waits for the individual to bring it forth by unraveling the mystery of the Divine

Self. Bring out the true, inner Self into the outward physical environment. LIGHT was and is the first creation of the Creator. LIGHT comes from the Creator. It was created and existed before I AM, before Spirit, before soul and before the physical body. From LIGHT came all great beings and LIGHT is at the essence and core of everything and all things.

LIGHT continues to expand outward. This process creates an endless space of energy and potentiality. It is inexhaustible. Yet most fail to use it because the mind is not open and the consciousness needs to expand.

The lesson is:
Learn to use the Conscious, Subconscious,
and Superconscious Minds in order to be
able to grow in awareness every day.

Five

Heaven and Earth have no preference
A man may choose one or the other
The Sage is like Heaven and Earth and has no
      preferences
He gives value to all people

The space between Heaven and Earth is like
      a bellows
empty yet inexhaustible
The more it is used the more it produces

People are not like this
They blow like a bellows in their intellectual
      discussions
and soon become exhausted
Man was not made to blow air like a bellows
He was created to still the mind
and discover the truth within

5

A person can choose to live in harmony with Universal Laws of the Mind or the choice can be made to live out of harmony with those Universal Laws. The result of the former is peace, fulfillment, love and enlightenment. The result of the latter is pain, discord, sorrow, hate and death.

A bellows constantly sucks air in from the outside environment and then blows that compressed air into a burning fire. Then the air is recirculated into the atmosphere. So it is with the Mind. Mind substance or Akasha constantly circulates from the inner levels of Mind to the outer physical universe and back again.

The movement of mind substance is directed by the thinker, the enlightened one in order to ensure that productive creations manifest in the physical environment which will be of value not only to the Self, but to all humanity.

Good and bad are ways in which the brain tries to place value on physical things. Heaven and Earth are neither good or bad because all Superconscious Mind, Subconscious Mind, and Conscious Mind exist for the evolution and development of I AM. Therefore, it is each person's duty to learn to use the total mind which includes Superconscious Mind symbolized by Heaven and Subconscious Mind symbolized by Earth in order to grow in consciousness.

The way we interpret experiences may be good or bad yet the experience is essentially neutral. The experience exists for our learning which is the learning of the soul. Learning for the soul is called Permanent Understandings of Self and Creation.

The Sage, the enlightened being, is neither good nor bad because such a one has risen in consciousness beyond the pairs of opposites called Maya. Maya is the word from India for these pairs of opposites.

This Maya or pairs of opposites is a function of existence in a physical body while receiving experiences through the five senses. The five senses of sight, smell, touch, taste, and hearing give us our view of the physical world. They inform the body and brain of hot or cold, pleasurable or painful. They also give us the mistaken impression that we are separate from the rest of the world. This is the great illusion. The true nature of reality is connectedness. We experience this connectedness when in love. We experience this connectedness when the mind is still.

The Sage, the enlightened being, is not limited by the brain. The Sage functions in all levels of Mind. The Sage uses the Mind to learn from and in every experience. The Sage recognizes the value in each soul and each experience.

Growing in consciousness is in large part a function of learning to move greater and greater amounts of energy through the Self. This recycling of energy is accomplished through the seven energy centers of the Self that are located near specific areas of the body. These energy centers are called chakras. The chakras act as energy transformers for the conscious, subconscious and superconscious minds of the Self.

The energy of the whole Mind, being infinite, is always present and available for one who has learned to still the Mind. As one grows in consciousness the energy of the whole Mind becomes more available. The duty of the Superconscious Mind is to give energy to the Subconscious and Conscious Minds. This life force energy is consistently given to one according to the capacity to receive it.

The more one uses the experience of life to build permanent soul understandings the more energy is available to use. Most people talk a lot or have busy thoughts that come mostly from their physical brains. Yet, this talking provides no opportunity for recycling used physical or Conscious Mind energy into the deeper levels of the Subconscious or Superconscious Mind. This is why they become exhausted.

18

The busy conscious mind that functions mostly in the physical brain will never gain the true fulfillment needed. Instead, a quiet and still mind is needed in order to know Self, know all of Mind, and gain enlightenment.

The lesson is:
Practice concentration exercises until the mind has become completely still. Then know the truth available in the inner levels of Mind, the Universal Truths.

Six

The valley spirit never dies
She is the original Mother
Her gateway reveals Heaven and Earth
Continuous and everlasting
like a veil barely seen
Use it
It is never exhausted

6

The valley spirit is the quality and power of receptivity. The aggressive quality and the receptive quality are the two great factors of creation.

A valley receives the water from the hills into its streams and rivers. To be receptive is to have learned the true art of causing receiving. All reaction is receptive to the Creator's Divine plan and thought energy. All of the Subconscious and Conscious Mind which includes the physical universe is receptive to the Superconscious Mind. The Superconscious Mind and Heaven are the same thing. Both are a state of consciousness rather than some place located a long distance away. Heaven is a state of consciousness, a place of supreme bliss and fulfillment. The Superconscious Mind is the source of all of Mind.

Superconscious Mind energy is ever present. It is called life force. Life force is usually not perceived by the five physical senses yet it is ever present and it is everywhere. As all life force continually recycles throughout all of mind it is always available. It is only the limited thinking in the conscious mind that limits one's ability to receive and use this boundless energy.

The valley spirit works through the Conscious Mind. The lowest part of mind where energy vibration is slowed down to a rate perceivable by the five senses as matter or substance or physical objects.

In the Bible, woman symbolizes the Conscious Mind. Mother Earth is the divine force of Creation manifested into the

21

physical plane or level of existence. This plane or level is also called the Conscious Mind.

The mother-woman also represents the receptive forces of creation. There are two aspects to any and all creations. The receptive-drawing quality and the aggressive-pushing quality or energy. The valley spirit is the I AM-soul entrapped in a physical body living out another of many lifetimes.

The Earth is our schoolroom. We must learn the lessons of divine love and Universal love, which are permanent and eternal, in order to progress to higher levels of consciousness.

Few understand how to use physical existence for true, lasting spiritual quickening. Few know how to lift this veil of darkness so as to enter into the greater LIGHT.

Those who learn to lift the veil of spiritual darkness to perceive the LIGHT of understanding will never want to go back to their old limited form of existence. All activity, all steps taken for soul growth, all time invested will always be worth the effort because what is gained is permanent and lasting. It is of the Divine and Eternal. It is of the High Self.

Those who thirst and desire for soul growth and high spiritual development and are willing to take action towards this end every day will not fail but will surely succeed. For behold, the Christ Consciousness stands at the door and knocks. To him who asks it shall be given. To him who knocks the door to the inner levels of consciousness will be opened (*Revelation 3:20, Matthew 7:7*).

The lesson is:
Receptivity is a powerful force.
Receptivity gives birth to all creation.
Cultivate receptivity and meditation,
with a still mind and
by listening.

Seven

Heaven is eternal and Earth endures
Why do Heaven and Earth continue and endure
It is because they do not live for themselves
Therefore they live on, continue and long endure

Therefore, the Sage chooses to be last
and thus becomes first
Surrenders Self
and Self is preserved and continues
Through Selfless action
fulfillment of his ideals is achieved

7

Heaven which is Superconscious Mind is eternal because it contains the perfect or Divine plan of creation. That plan is for all I AM's to become enlightened and compatible to their Creator. *Genesis 1:26* of the Bible says; *"Then God said, 'Let us make man in our image, after our likeness'."* To make in our image is to use the imagination effectively.

Image = Imagination or directed visualization

After our likeness means or indicates to have like or similar attributes. Therefore, the plan in Superconscious Mind is for all I AM's or souls to fully gain in consciousness and manifest the full and enlightened understanding of Self as a Creator.

A creator uses the image-making capacity to move the consciousness forward.

I AM manifests as Spirit or the Real Self in Superconscious Mind. I AM manifests as soul in Subconscious Mind. I AM manifests as the physical body, brain and the conscious ego in the Conscious Mind.

Earth also continues in order that all souls will be able to incarn in physical bodies in order to build permanent understandings of Self and creation and mature as enlightened beings. The more one lives the life to aid others with the awareness and wisdom one has built the more rapid will one progress into enlightenment as the Dharma or duty of the Self is fulfilled.

Dharma is a word from India meaning the duty one has to teach – to give to and to aid – the rest of humanity to grow in enlightenment. Thus does one build a continual, connected consciousness.

To choose to be last is to serve others. It is true that *"as you give so shall you receive" (Matthew 7:12)*. The one who surrenders Self is the one who gives to others and aids others in the highest way known. The ability to aid others as if they are the

Self eliminates separation and enables one to live in harmony with the true nature of the universe and all of Mind which is connectedness. The greater one builds this awareness of connectedness the more one will come to know oneness in Self.

To know oneness or connectedness in Self is to know connectedness and oneness with all creation. It is living the true nature of reality.

The enlightened one is a thinker. He perceives the way life, people, and the earth are moving. Then he makes a decision to move forward in consciousness. Creation is continual. Therefore, creation is forever and eternal. Heaven and Earth are two ends of the same creation. Heaven is Superconscious Mind. Earth is the Subconscious and Conscious Minds. Since creation is continual and eternal it has neither beginning or end. The concepts of beginning and ending are horizontal, physical, thinking which are ruled by physical time.

Creation is beyond physical time, space, and substance. Creation is vertical time. Creation is mental and can become physically manifested on earth. The Sage is living because he is a creator. He is continually producing forward motion, learning and soul growth.

The enlightened one is detached, and can expand the consciousness to all things and beings, and all creations. One who is emotionally attached is always limited in consciousness to that which one is attached to.

Selfless action produces and expands consciousness. Sacred service or selfless action reaches out to help, aid and teach others to grow, prosper, and gain enlightenment.

As you give you shall receive. Through selfless action in aiding and giving to others the Sage receives every good thing the universe has to offer for this is the Universal Law of Abundance.

Thus the Sage gains universal connectedness and achieves spiritual ideals.

The lesson is:
Be disciplined and constantly give to others.

Eight

The best way to live is to be like water
for water benefits all things
without competing or going against anything
flowing in places others reject and avoid
This is why water is like the Tao

Dwell close to the Earth
still the mind thoughts and go deep
Give with kindness
speak truth and honesty
govern peacefully
be responsible when serving others
when causing movement be timely

Such a one does not go against the nature of things
Therefore, things do not go against such a one

8

Water flows. Water fills spaces. After air, water is the substance our physical bodies need most. Without water, physical life as we know it would not exist on this planet. Truly water brings life to all. It is because of these functions that water appears as conscious life experience in our night dreams. When water is prominent in a night dream it symbolizes the dreamer's previous day's experiences. These experiences were received by the conscious mind. Hence, the term conscious life experiences.

Water flows into swamps. Water will flow into a cup. Water will flow downhill because of gravity. Water flows into empty spaces. It does so naturally. People also function best when they flow, when they do not avoid learning opportunities, and when they fill in the spaces created for them. In this manner water is a fitting analogy for the Tao, the Way.

Just as the water dwells close to the earth in streams, ponds, rivers and oceans, so also it is important for each person to align or use their conscious mind to dwell close to the subconscious mind. For water symbolizes conscious life experiences and earth symbolizes subconscious mind substance.

As one develops – through concentration and meditation – the ability to still the mind then one can dive deep into the inner levels of consciousness finally achieving superconscious awareness.

The more enlightened one becomes, the more connected one is with all people, all things, and all creation. Kindness connects the Self with others. Truth and honesty connects one with the Universal Truths and Universal Laws and thereby with everyone and everything.

To govern peacefully is to be in harmony with all of nature and all of creation. This is being responsible.

All actions, all effort, all activity is to be used in such a way that students of the Mind may learn to act more and more in accord with the Universal Law and Universal Truth. The more one is in harmony by having a still mind and living in truth the more one will know the correct time to act, speak and receive. When a person is in harmony with the Self and the Mind then one also cooperates with the energy, action and form that is already in motion in nature and the world. Therefore, all and everything naturally harmonizes with such a one.

Water flows. Water assumes the form needed. Water gives life. Water is flexible, not rigid.

The highest good flows. The highest good assumes the form needed. The highest good gives life. The highest good always responds creating the form needed to create and advance the cause of humanity's evolution. The highest good assumes a form in order to create and add to evolution. When the form is no longer used for the highest good the form dissolves back into Subconscious Mind substance and a new form is created, a form more needed by humanity in the present.

Be in tune and in harmony with Universal Laws and their manifestations in our physical environment and life. Be attuned to Mother Nature as She it was who gave us the physical body. Nature is alive. We can receive this aliveness from nature. Trees are our friends. When you touch a tree you openly receive life. Meditation is achieved by the still mind. In the still and quiet mind we receive and identify truth. Then we live truth which is added as permanent LIGHT to our consciousness.

As you do unto others so you do unto yourself. As you do to yourself so you do to others.

Gentleness and kindness are the ways in which one desires to be treated. The kindness with which you desire to be treated is the kindness you need to give to others. This produces connectedness. Connectedness is the natural order of the universe. Connectedness is of the nature of the Conscious and Subconscious Minds. Interconnectedness leads to oneness or unity consciousness which is attuned to Superconscious Mind. Cause your words and thoughts to match. Cause your words and mental pictures to match. Cause your words, thoughts and actions to align. Then you live in truth and LIGHT.

In directing others or directing the many aspects of Self work from cause to effect. Thought is cause. Effect is the physical manifestation or form coming from the mental thought cause. This is power.

In dealing with others always produce more than you consume. This is adulthood of reasoning.

It is by stilling the mind and aligning with vertical time that perfect timing is achieved. The correct timing is always dependent on the mental attitude. One who fights against the universe always loses because the universe and its Creator is all powerful. Therefore, align the consciousness with Universal Law.

True responsibility is achieved when there is no blame. A mental adult is responsible. The reasoner accepts the fact that one's thoughts and attitudes determines one's life.

The lesson is:
Be receptive to life and learn to flow with it.

Nine

Instead of grabbing and hoarding
stop while you can
Over sharpen the blade
and the edge will not last long
Amass rooms full of gold and jade
and no one will be able to protect it

Fill yourself with pride and vanity and
bring about one's own downfall
Complete the task in which you are engaged
be selfless in your actions
this is the Way of Heaven

9

Physical objects and physical sensory experience will never bring lasting happiness or fulfillment. It is only through the use of physical sensory experience to determine the lesson of life that the thinker comes to know self, as an eternal being of LIGHT.

The more one hoards objects, the more attention is bound up in those objects. Yet the nature of Mind is to expand, to grow, to add to the awareness of Self.

Therefore, it is important to remember that all physical experiences and objects are temporary. They will all pass away. The Sage, the thinker, the enlightened individual will glean the permanent understandings of Self and creation from the experience.

The analogy of over sharpening a blade is appropriate. An over sharpened blade dulls easily. A person who over amasses objects, memories, or emotional attachments will also dull the ability to reason and to gain awareness in all situations and circumstances.

The same message is presented in regard to gold and jade. Jade was very highly prized in ancient China much as diamonds are in the present time period. Since all physical experiences are temporary it is impossible to hold permanently onto them. Even if a person could hold onto a large amount of physical objects, he still will lose them at the point of death. Physical objects and physical experiences are by their very nature temporary. To try to make them permanent is a self defeating attitude. Therefore, it is up to us to do as the Master Jesus of Nazareth commanded. *"Do not store up for yourself treasures buried in the ground, a place where rust and moths destroy and where thieves break through and steal. Rather, lay up for yourselves a treasure in heaven, where neither rust nor moths destroy and where thieves do not break through and steal. For where your treasure is, there also is your heart" (Matthew 6: 19, 20).*

Heaven symbolizes Superconscious Mind. The one who aligns the Conscious and Subconscious Minds through the discipline of concentration and meditation and who uses this discipline to discern the permanent learning of Universal Truth and Universal Law in every situation is the one who attunes to Superconscious Mind and lays up treasures of Self awareness and cosmic consciousness.

To fill the Self with pride and vanity is to misuse the conscious ego. It is to have an over-inflated ego. It is to have a dishonest conscious mind and a dishonest conscious ego.
The conscious ego is designed to be the motivator of the Self. The one who is not constantly motivated to improve the Self is the one who is not using the ego correctly.

Since the conscious ego's function is not to reason but to motivate, to allow the conscious ego to run the life will always lead to many mistakes and errors in judgement that bring about one's downfall.

By completing the task in which you are engaged one has the opportunity to understand one's creations from beginning to completion. Therefore, the opportunity exists to add to the permanent soul understandings of Self and Creation stored in one's soul or subconscious Mind.

The true nature of reality and of all of creation is connectedness. Selfless action for the purpose of aiding others, connects one to others in greater and greater ways. Since the way of Heaven which is Superconscious Mind is connectedness, the one who practices connectedness through selfless action comes to know Heaven and exists in Superconscious Mind. Such a one's conscious ego has been transformed into I AM consciousness.

In order to receive continually, one must give continually. When one continually takes and refuses to give, the inner cup of Self fills making it impossible to receive more.

The average person is under the power of the pairs of opposites. The pairs of opposites entrap people in the five senses and keep them engrossed in physical forms and limitation. Rather than go to extremes instead strive to have a peaceful, balanced mind that continually uses the aggressive and receptive principles in balance. Perfection is not to be found in the physical existence. It is but a reflection of the greater or High Self and Superconscious Mind.

Physical forms deteriorate. They begin this rotting process as soon as they manifest or appear in the physical environment.

True everlasting wealth is accumulated through Truth and Love. Together they give the individual LIGHT.

Tie your attention, time, and effort to temporary things and you will become temporary and finite instead of eternal and infinite. Instead, cultivate and use the still and quiet mind to assimilate the soul learning from each action and each experience.

The still and quiet Conscious Mind aligned with Subconscious Mind and attuned to Superconscious Mind is the way to have Heaven on Earth.

The lesson is:

Include others in one's creations and successes.

Ten

As a soul inhabiting a physical body

Can you still the mind, embrace the original
oneness and keep them from separating
Can you concentrate the vital breath until
softness in Self is achieved
Can you be like a newborn baby
Can you purify the mirror of inner perception
until Self is perceived clearly
Can you serve and govern people
without imposing your will
Can you be like the female and receptively open
and close the gates of heaven
Can you still the mind and be open to all things
and thus become the Light of the World

Giving birth and nourishing
Giving birth without possessing
Leading without controlling
This is the mysterious power

You are a soul inhabiting a physical body. You are not the physical body. The physical body is temporary just as all physical things are temporary. Just as the physical body is a vehicle for the Real Self so also is the mind. Mind is the vehicle I AM uses in order to learn to be a creator. In order for a soul existing in a physical body to know I AM one must bring the restless mind of Self under control. One must still the thoughts of the mind in order to perceive deeply into the true meaning of Self and creation.

When we were created we experienced oneness with the Creator and all creation. Yet, needing to gain experience we entered all of Mind, the Superconscious, the Subconscious or Universal Mind, and finally the Conscious mind and physical world. This movement away from LIGHT to physical existence caused or brought about the illusion of distance or separation. This illusion of separation is called Maya.

In our physical world this illusion of separateness is brought on by the five physical senses. For example, the sense of sight tells us we are separate from the object we are seeing. What we are seeing is in fact a reflected LIGHT image.

One avoids this illusion of separateness by stilling the mind, concentrating the breath or concentrating on one's breath until the breath is the connected breath of a newborn baby. Then you are ready to perceive accurately for past memories and sensory input no longer obstruct the perception of the Real Self and the true nature of reality.

Then one is ready and able to serve humanity, teach and lead them to a higher state of consciousness for such a one has already led the 144,000 aspects of Self to Higher Consciousness.

Then the enlightened one can lead by Love, Truth, and LIGHT instead of force of will.

In order to enter the Superconscious Mind which is Heaven one must become receptive. One must master the receptive quality for only one who is able to receive the truth of connectedness leading to oneness will harmonize with the vibration of connectedness in Superconscious Mind.

A female body is by nature receptive. A soul that chooses a female physical body to incarn into desires the perspective of receptivity. True and great receptivity comes as one masters and learns to still the mind. The one who can be receptive and receive the LIGHT of Heaven-Superconscious Mind is the one who can give the LIGHT to the world. Such a one is the LIGHT of the world. In the Bible *Book of Matthew,* Jesus says to his disciples, *"You are the LIGHT of the World; a city that is built up on a mountain cannot be hidden."*

Birth, interpreted in dream symbols and the Universal Language of Mind, symbolizes a new idea being brought forth. A new and more enlightened idea of Self is necessary in order to grow into enlightenment. This idea must be nurtured. Nourishing must be done without trying to limit, restrict, or control. The new, higher image of the Self must be employed as a moving image or picture that is constantly in motion moving ever forward and evolving. A stagnant picture will not suffice. This ability to nurture and grow is the greatest virtue, the greatest ability and the greatest learning.

You are an I AM, an identity, an individuality. I AM that is the individuality expresses in Superconscious Mind as Spirit or High Self, in Subconscious Mind as soul and in the Conscious Mind as the physical body. You have a physical body. You as an I AM wear a physical body and a soul. As you strive to unite body, soul and High Self you become one with Creator, all Creation and all aspects of Self. It is possible.

Then will you avoid the separation that physical entrapment and engrossment in the five senses imposes upon the person.

You must learn to give your undivided attention fully while remaining flexible and responsive to change. The thinker causes change. This series of caused changes evolves into the overcoming of imagined limitations and the expansion of consciousness.

Such a one is as a newborn babe fully absorbing all experiences – mental, emotional and physical. Such a one has no blockages to receiving mental thoughts, emotions or physical actions and words.

Mental perception existed before engrossment in the five senses and will exist after and beyond entrapment in the physical existence, and engrossment in the five physical senses. The perception will expand and evolve to superconsciousness. Then your thoughts will be clear, pure and directed.

To love everyone and everything is to be connected and without fear. Through love one comes to know all aspects of Self.

Heaven is Superconscious Mind. To open and close the gates of Heaven is to learn to enter Superconscious Mind while still existing in a physical body.

The Superconscious Mind must be entered receptively, not aggressively. This is why being like a female is required. You cannot conquer Superconscious Mind. You can receive Superconscious awareness into yourself.

To have super knowledge which is power and super openness which is the ability to receive all knowledge, wisdom and experience is to remain centered in your being, with the still, quiet mind while not being engrossed in physical experiences.

Give birth to a new expanded consciousness and eternal connected consciousness. Nourish this connected consciousness into Superconscious, unity consciousness. Give birth to new creations, yet expand beyond the need to be engrossed in your creations. Thereby you glean the full learning from all experience.

Activity is to be done for soul growth and spiritual development.

When activity is done to feed the conscious ego then the soul does not progress for the conscious ego self has already received a physical reward. Such a one has settled for less than permanent understandings which are soul growth and the fulfillment of the assignment.

To lead is to have a clear mental image and communicate that image to all aspects of Self and others. Thereby all can work toward a common goal and ideal.

One leads because of vision and communicating that vision of the future, of what can be. Then there can be cooperation toward a common ideal. Then all can fulfill the soul urge.

The lesson is:

Give, receive, nourish and create and gain the power of an enlightened being.

Eleven

Thirty spokes unite in the hub of the wheel
It is the emptiness of the center whole
that makes it useful

Shape clay into a bowl
It is the space within that allows it to be useful

Cut out doors and windows for a house
These created openings of space give it usefulness

Thus, physical form is beneficial
Its usefulness comes from creating a space

There are two great principles of creation. The inbreath of God (Brahm) and the outbreath of God (Brahm).

The inbreath is the receptive principle. The outbreath is the aggressive principle. The two are also referred to as Yin and Yang. Receptivity is creating a space to receive. Receptivity is expectant non-action.

Nature rushes to fill a space. The space or hole draws all to it. Without space there is no-thing.

The number 30 is made of the numbers 3 and 0. Three is the number of creation symbolized in Holy Books as Father, Mother, Child. Zero indicates the power that comes from knowledge and understanding. Power, knowledge, and creativity become useful when they have a space in which to operate.

Clay represents all substance of Mind. This substance of Subconscious Mind is known as Akasha. In the physical environment it manifests as physical objects.

A space is created by a directing mind. Clay is molded by a directing mind. The one who applies receptivity to create a space is the directing Mind. Such a one has power.

Windows and doors represent openings to the mind and soul. The holes let in the LIGHT and people. It is receptivity that draws the LIGHT of awareness to the Self. It is receptivity that brings all aspects of Self together in harmony. It is receptivity that draws all things together.

Holes are spaces that have yet to be filled.

The physical body we inhabit and our physical world in all its myriad of shapes and forms, gives us the place to build soul understanding. Great is the benefit to one who fills the holy space.

Usefulness comes from what or who creates the Hole or Whole Space. To create a space is to have the opportunity to receive the new learning for the whole Self.

Form is from below. Usefulness is from above. No man can serve two masters. Either he serves the Creator-High Self and Superconscious Mind or he serves money, physical entrapment and the conscious ego-devil.

The lesson is:
Create a space

to learn
by having a still
and open mind.

Twelve

The five colors blind the eyes
The five tones deafen the ears
The five tastes numb the mouth
Racing thoughts weaken the mind
Constantly pursuing engrossing physical desires
slows the motion to enlightenment

Therefore, the Sage is not concerned with the pull
of the senses
and is guided by the needs of the inner Self
Thus he chooses what is deep
and not what lies on the surface

Engrossment in the senses dulls the mind. One may get so caught up in the senses that the truth and soul learning in the experience is missed. The purpose of life is not sensory experiences. The purpose of life is to use our physical, sensory experiences to build permanent understanding and higher consciousness of Self and creation.

When the mind is racing and the thoughts are jumping from one object to another the Self is out of control. This leads to anger and sadness. Attractive, eye catching objects lead one astray from the real object of life which is to learn and grow in soul awareness.

The mind is not designed to engross the Self in experience. The mind is designed to give the Self a wonderful place to build permanent soul learning called understandings. In order to accomplish this the reasoner must discipline the mind and bring it under control. This can be accomplished with concentration and meditation. Therefore, the thinker, the reasoner trusts and listens to the inner Self for the senses can be misleading. The senses can lie to a person. However, the inner voice of the soul will always present truth.

The enlightened one, the Sage, lets go of sensory and emotional attachments and chooses what is permanent, lasting, eternal and real. Such a one listens to the inner Self and acts on these perceptions.

Soul growth, spiritual development and permanent understanding of eternal love and truth and LIGHT are what the wise one chooses.

The secret truths of creation, the knowledge of the Real Self, the awareness of all levels of mind and cosmic consciousness come to the one who chooses what is deep. What lies on the surface is physical, sensory experiences which are transitory. Therefore, look to perceive the deeper meaning in all experiences. Be disciplined to gain awareness of the soul, the spirit and the I AM.

The lesson is:

***Receive with the senses.
Perceive with the Mind. Learn
Single-pointed concentration and
know the deeper reality.***

Thirteen

Recognize favor and disgrace as a warning
Honor and affliction are tied to the body

Why recognize favor and disgrace as a warning?
Favor makes one inferior
     gain favor with apprehension
     lose favor with apprehension
     Therefore, be wary of both favor and disgrace

Why is affliction tied to the body or a limited sense
     of Self?
The reason one has afflictions
     is because one is entrapped in a physical body
Without the soul's entrapment in a physical body
     what afflictions would one possess?

Therefore, the one who appreciates his
     connectedness with everything
     can be entrusted with the world
The one who loves Self as
     connected with everyone
     is ready to be a teacher of the world

Both favor and disgrace are based upon external factors. To gain favor is for someone else to look favorably upon you. To be disgraced is for others to view you unfavorably.

Honor and disaster, favor and disgrace are like the physical body in that they are temporary. To seek the favor from others is to place one's value outside of the Self. This is why favor makes one inferior. One needs to use the physical environment and world to raise the consciousness, to ascend in consciousness.

One day you may be in favor with others in the environment. The next day you may be out of favor. It is all temporary. The soul needs permanent and eternal soul understandings added to the Self. Temporary sensory experiences will not do. Disaster or affliction is like the physical body because both are temporary and are of the nature of physical existence.

Before incarning in a physical body and between lifetimes the soul has no distress or affliction. The soul has needs. The soul attempts through incarnations to fulfill these needs for soul growth and spiritual development.

The one who identifies with Self as a soul existing in Subconscious or Universal Mind recognizes the truth that everything and everyone is connected. The more one grows into Superconscious awareness, the more one understands, exists in, and fulfills this universal connectedness that leads to a singular or unified consciousness.

Such a one can be entrusted with the world because it is understood and perceived that everything is connected to the Self and Self is intimately connected with everything. This gives greater meaning to the Biblical phrase by Jesus, *"Do unto others as you would have them do unto you" (Matthew 7:12).* Also, *"Love your neighbor as yourself" (Matthew 22:39).*

From this, one is ready to be a Master teacher as was and is Lao Tzu and Jesus who gained the Christ Consciousness. Such a one is a teacher for the world. Such a one's consciousness encompasses the entire planet Earth.

Physical losses or gains are temporary. Add to the Self what is permanent and everlasting. Accept the truth that each one is on this earth to produce permanent understandings of Self, Love, and LIGHT, Truth and Creation. All else is limited and temporary.

Misfortune or affliction is inherent in the fact we exist in a limited form called a physical body. Misfortune is indicated due to the condition of being entrapped in a physical body and on the cycle of reincarnation. Physical existence is limited. Physical perception is limited to the five senses. The nature of the physical is inertia. The strangeness of the physical life is indicated by the duration of time required for thought to manifest in a person's life. Often by the time a thought has solidified or manifested into physical form, the individual does not even remember the thought that created the form and condition.

The Self is an energy being. The Self in a physical body accepts the limitations of dense form and structure and slowed down vibration or energy. The illumined soul is energy, vibration and creation that is free. Such an individual can be trusted to do God's will which is limitless creation, infinite love, and eternal life.

Bring this Love of the Creator fully into your being, then you can Love your neighbor as yourself.

With Universal Love the Self does good for all mankind, all Earth and all Creation.

With Infinite Love the Self aids all creation. The energy being is filled with LIGHT and becomes a master teacher, a world savior.

The lesson is:

Avoid dependency upon temporary, physical objects and circumstances concerning one's mental peace and well-being.
Gain peace and connectedness.

Fourteen

We look but do not see it because it is beyond sight
We listen but do not hear it because it is beyond
sound
We reach but do not grasp it because it is beyond
the senses
It is the connectedness of oneness

Oneness –
there is nothing more enlightening above it
and nothing less enlightening below it
A continuous thread beyond creation
It returns to Light consciousness
before form and substance
This is the form of the yet to be formed
The image yet to be shaped into substance
It is subtle and elusive
Stand before it and you will not know its beginning
Follow it and you will not discover its ending
Be still and exist in the eternal now
The ancient Way is to master the present, eternal
now
To know all in the eternal now
is the Key to the Tao's continuity

The energy of Creation exists in Superconscious Mind. It moves into Subconscious Mind and then Conscious Mind.

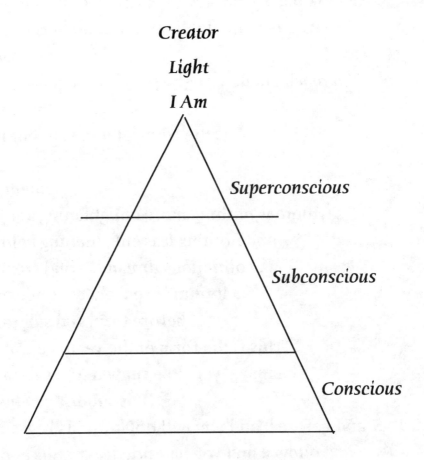

The Conscious Mind may be termed physical existence or the physical environment.

The five senses of touch, taste, smell, hearing and sight are vehicles the soul uses to experience while in a physical body. The five senses are designed to receive these mental images, these electro-chemical sensory experiences from the physical environment.

The five senses are not designed to receive or interpret the higher vibration of the Subconscious Mind or the Superconscious Mind.

One who relies solely on the five senses for experience and thinking, is limited in thinking and is physically engrossed in matter.

In Subconscious Mind all souls are interconnected. This becomes apparent as one becomes highly developed spiritually.

In Superconscious Mind there is a oneness of unity of consciousness. This too is experienced and understood by the highly spiritualized beings. We only know brightness when we identify with darkness. Bright and dark are the pairs of opposites that keep Self entrapped in physical existence. The goal is to move into the LIGHT, to raise one's vibrations to be LIGHT. Then there is no overpowering brightness or darkness. Instead all is filled with LIGHT and Love.

Thought forms are images that are created, released, shaped and move from the conscious mind of the individual to the subconscious mind. There the thought form gathers mind substance. When it gains enough substance it manifests outward into the physical existence as a part of our experience and environment.

Life force from Superconscious Mind also moves out into physical existence constantly. Yet, it is beyond the capability of the physical senses to perceive its source.

Instead of identifying with horizontal, physical time, place your attention and awareness on vertical time which is mental and spiritual time. Instead of measuring time as a sequence of events, the spiritualized soul learns to know time as duration and the movement of the soul forward into richer spirituality and more expanded consciousness.

There is no beginning to creation and no end to creation because creation exists beyond and above physical time. Creation is continual.

Be one with eternal creation. Know eternal creation by being a creator. Exist fully in the now. It is in the eternal now that the Self will know eternal and continual creation. The phrase be still and exist in the eternal now is like the Bible which says, *"Be still and know that I AM God."*

Thus you will come to know Creator and creation. When you know creation and creator you will experience, understand, and know the cause of creation. You will know the essence of Creator all in the eternal now.

The key to the Tao is to exist fully in the eternal present now.

The lesson is:

Cause the attention to be in the present and create the future.

Fifteen

The enlightened Masters of the ancient path
are receptive, simple, and expansive in their
consciousness
Deep in their understanding and wise in their giving
Most people are not capable of understanding
the enlightened Master's high consciousness
Because of this I will describe their outer form or
presentation
Observant, as if crossing a river in winter
Alert as one in enemy territory
Reverent as if receiving an honored guest
Yielding as the melting ice
Simple like uncarved wood
Receptive and open like a valley
Murky like puddles of water
The water of the puddle becomes clear when it is still
Being of still mind one causes motion of life
Such a one fulfills the Tao yet never fills up
A continuous cycle that brings everlasting life

What are the qualities of an enlightened being? How shall a person recognize such a one? The three factors or qualities that may be described as receptive, simple, and expansive are useful and accurate.

A person does not become enlightened by being closed off. One becomes enlightened rapidly by opening the mind to receive the learning in every experience. To be receptive is to have command and use of the ability to receive. To be simple is to function from higher levels of Mind and higher planes of existence where the universal connectedness of all creation is perceived and apparent.

To live a complicated life is to function mostly from the brain and 5 senses. The senses give the illusion that everything is separate from the Self. One cannot possibly understand the life when everything is separate from the Self for it gets too complicated. The only way one can understand the Self, the life, and all the universe is to raise the consciousness to perceive connectedness.

We experience physical life as complicated. This is because physical existence is the division of Mind farthest removed from our source as LIGHT. In the physical world LIGHT's vibration is slowed down so we may experience matter with the five senses. The senses deceive the person and make it seem as if one is separate from everything else. Other people, places, and things are perceived as separate and apart from Self. Therefore, the one living in the illusionary world of the senses views the world as segmented, fragmented, and disjointed.

The masters of consciousness knew all life to be connected. Therefore, the more Subconscious and Superconscious Minds are known, the more everything is seen and understood to be connected in a unity and therefore simple.

Consciousness is not physical matter. Mind is not physical substance. Although these are a part of it. The masters of Mind exist, with awareness on many different levels of Mind simultaneously.

The one with the quiet, still mind perceives clearly as the muddy consciousness clears. Such a one knows how and when to respond. The masters of consciousness build permanent understandings of Creation in the Self. The physical world of temporary desires and stimuli do not distract them from their goal of enlightenment for the entire human race. As one goes beyond the confines of the five senses and the physical body, the expansiveness of the Mind is perceived. As one progresses in soul learning the consciousness of Self expands to fill all of Mind.

An enlightened being is observant because the senses and mind have been mastered. Such a one can give full and undivided attention to the person or object of focus and concentration.

Such a one is alert because the perception, will, and attention have been highly developed through years or lifetimes of mental and Spiritual disciplines. An enlightened being is reverent because there is the full comprehension of the connectedness of Self with all beings and the appreciation of the value of all experiences one draws to the Self.

Such a one is yielding because creation is constantly changing. Therefore, to be fixed or stubborn is to miss out on learning. Such a one is murky because the average, sensory, engrossed person cannot perceive the depths of an enlightened being's consciousness.

The enlightened being quiets the restless thoughts and stills the mind.

The Dhammapada, Chapter 3 verse 37 says, *"Those who can direct thoughts, which are unsubstantial and wander so aimlessly are freed from the bonds of Mara."* Verse 38, *"They are wise whose thoughts are steady and minds serene, unaffected by good and bad."* The Dhammapada or Dharmapada is a collection, a record of the sayings of Gautama the Buddha, one of the most enlightened beings to ever walk the face of the planet Earth.

The lesson is:

It is through a still mind that one fulfills the Tao.
The one with a still mind becomes a being of
LIGHT
and exists in the continual, ever lasting life
of full awareness and consciousness.

In the still mind resides receptivity.

Sixteen

Cause the mind of Self to be empty and open
The center of being to be still
Then you will be able to perceive
the ten thousand events that rise connected
Experiences and things grow and flourish in endless
variation
and then once again return to the source
The source is stillness
From stillness comes the cycles of creation
From stillness they come alive
Alive and in motion in the continuum of
consciousness
To know consciousness is known as enlightenment
To not know consciousness leads to misery and error
To maintain an all encompassing, expanded
consciousness leads to an open mind
The open mind leads to an open heart
To be openhearted is to gain rulership of Self
To rule is to be like Heaven
To be like Heaven is to be one with the Tao
To be one with the Tao is to maintain an eternal life
of connected consciousness free from exhaustion

First the student needs to practice the mental discipline of concentration. Then the student progresses through meditation to a still Mind. As the student teaches and integrates the higher consciousness the Mind becomes empty. Then one can cause a stillness at any time.

The Mind can be stilled more easily because the thinker is not fighting against the thoughts that need to be shared. One who has practiced mental discipline can then cause the Mind to be still. Achieve a state of no thought. This requires mental discipline. When the Mind is still the Self gains peace and the Mind opens.

When the Mind is still, the Self becomes aware of the many aspects of one's conscious and subconscious minds.

When the Mind becomes empty, the Self becomes the observer. Being the observer such a one is able to observe how thoughts are created in the Conscious Mind, then move to Subconscious or Universal Mind where they gain substance and form. These thoughts then may manifest as thousands or tens of thousands of different objects and events in one's life. Then these solid thought forms deteriorate and return to Subconscious Mind substance from which they came.

The source of all creation is the Creator. From the Creator issued forth LIGHT. The eternal Creator can be known in the space between thoughts. The eternal Creator can be known in the peace and stillness between thoughts. Therefore, extend the space and time between thoughts.

Thought is the way of creating. Thought is a motion in creation. Knowing how to achieve peace while creating or in creation is awareness. One who fails to harmonize with creation in motion invites pain because such a one fails to harmonize with Universal Law which is creation already in motion.

Knowing the motion of creation one is open to change and causes transformation instead of fearing change. From the self-security which comes from open mindness one gains an open heart.

All creation comes from thought. Each person is constantly creating his or her life by the thoughts created by the Self.

From a still mind issues forth thought. These thoughts are alive and in motion. These thoughts are often connected to other thoughts. To maintain full awareness and consciousness is a choice to still the Mind and exist in the present moment.

In order for a cup to fully receive, it must be empty. In order for the Self to fully receive, the Mind must be empty.

To lack awareness of one's own thoughts and the effects they create is to make mistakes that create pain and suffering. The Dharmapada of Gautama the Buddha, Chapter 1, verse 1 and 2 says: *"Our life is shaped by our mind; we become what we think. Suffering follows an evil thought as the wheels of a cart follow the oxen that draw it. Our life is shaped by our mind; we become what we think. Joy follows a pure thought like a shadow that never leaves."*

The open Mind allows one to receive. To be able to receive enables one to receive the LIGHT, truth, and understanding into the heart.

The open hearted one is full of love. The open hearted one gives love freely. The open hearted one is thus a royal benefactor and divine. Being a divine giver and receiver of Love such a person experiences oneness with the Creator's Creation. Such a one is in harmony with the love and LIGHT of the Universe.

Creation is eternal. The one who aligns with and is consciously connected to Divine Creation is immortal and full of light. Though the physical Earth and environment changes and people, places and things come and go, continual creation has no ending. It is time–less and eternal. The enlightened being, the one full of LIGHT, is eternally conscious and aware.

The lesson is:

The still mind is an open mind and leads to an empty mind. Cultivate an open mind and an open heart. An open heart leads to understanding. Share your thoughts and empty the mind.

59

Seventeen

The Highest type of ruler
is the one of whose existence the people are barely
      aware
Next comes the ruler whom they love and respect
Next comes the ruler whom they fear
Next comes the ruler they hate and defy
If the ruler does not trust the self
there will be no trust in the ruler
Therefore,
The Sage chooses words carefully
when his efforts succeed and things have been
      completed
He lets the people think they caused it

17

The one who is fulfilling the soul assignment and growing into LIGHT has a Self value and worth that is not dependent upon what others think or say about the Self.

Next comes the leader who many love and respect. Love and respect are valuable attributes. Freely giving of the highest good is not designed to be done for the purpose of what you can receive from others. Rather it is to be done in order that one may receive of the abundance and enlightenment of the Universe.

Few people have as their goal in life to know the Self. Fewer still who give their whole life's work to gain enlightenment. Fewer still who aid many others to gain enlightenment.

When one begins the process of quickening the soul growth and spiritual development, fulfillment is experienced as the soul is nourished. A great love is also received as the eager student aligns the inner and outer, the Conscious and Subconscious Minds.

Such a one also draws to the Self people of like mind. In this there is also greater fulfillment and love.

Birds of a feather flock together and people with strong spiritual yearnings and urgings are drawn to each other through the Universal Law of Attraction.

Following this the Self becomes aware of the limitations received and learned in the brain and conscious mind from parents, relatives, teachers and others in the environment.

These learning limitations create fear, for fear comes from the unknown. These fears must be overcome in order for the mind and consciousness to expand beyond previously held forms and mental concepts that are outgrown and therefore limiting. Any angers or hatred that are re-actions to the limitations of fear also arise in order that Self may be fully aware of the limitations in consciousness and move beyond them.

The one who does not trust Self and Self's intentions will not trust others because such a one mistakenly thinks other people think like oneself. When in truth everyone thinks differently.

If you want to be trusted you must be trustworthy. Whatever you desire to receive from others you must first give of that from yourself.

Trust comes from inner security, honesty, and integrity. It is in alignment with the universal principles of Love and Truth.

The one who is secure in the Self and has a surrendered ego does not need to brag about accomplishments. Such a one does everything for soul growth, not for accolades from others.

Those who have yet to master their conscious ego want to take credit as a sort of validation of their importance and worth.

The soul progressing individual is steadily and daily making rapid progress in internalizing self worth, respect, and security independent of any person, place or thing.

The lesson is:

Create for the purpose of learning to be a creator and to aid others. Outward glorification is temporary. Value and importance come from what you give and in this way receive. Value and importance do not come from what you control or from how much praise one receives.

Eighteen

When the Great Tao is abandoned
rules of kindness and justice arise
When cunning and intellect appear
the great deceit begins
When the family lacks harmony
then we hear of dutiful children
When the state is in disorder and decay
then we hear of loyal ministers

18

The Great Way is the Tao, the way of LIGHT and awareness.
Life in our physical world is to be used as a schoolroom for soul
learning and understanding the secrets of creation.

When people forget how to be mental creators, when
people are no longer in touch with the source of creation, when
people think only physically instead of mentally, then they think
they are separate from everything and everyone else. Being separate and disjointed, they try to find ways to get along with other
people. Kindness and justice then are used as ways to be connected with others even though the real source of
interconnectedness is forgotten.

When people become separate from creation they become
insecure and therefore attempt to dominate their environment-
creation. As a poor substitute for experiencing the power of being connected to all of creation these entrapped and separated
people attempt to use the brain to learn to dominate the environment. This higher use of the brain is called intelligence, cunning,
intellect or being smart. However, living in the brain instead of
the mind creates insecurity.

Being separate these ones are still insecure. They therefore pretend to be something they are not. There is a tendency
to try to hide or cover up the insecurities that come from being
disconnected from others and all of creation.

When there is no peace within the Self there is the search-
ing and seeking for peace and harmony outside of Self.

When the Self is confused and the life is in chaos because
of the separation caused by engrossment in the senses and brain,
then the person grabs hold of some idea, some thing or some
person to be loyal to as a means of gaining exterior security.

Such a one needs to learn to still the restless mind, learn to meditate, learn to be connected with others through love and truth in order that the consciousness can be expanded into the LIGHT.

The soul exists in a physical body for the purpose of building permanent understandings of the Self and creation. This includes the Universal Truths and Universal Laws. Only by focusing on the learning or understanding that is for the soul will one find true and lasting happiness, peace and fulfillment.

The lesson is:

Live in connectedness realizing everything you think, do, and say affects everyone else. Whatever you wish others to do for you, do likewise also for them.

Nineteen

Eliminate smartness and intellectualism
and people will live a hundred times better
Eliminate benevolence and morality
and the people will return to compassion and
devotion
Eliminate cleverness and profit
then stealing and theft will disappear

These three remedies treat outward forms only
they are not the complete and whole teachings
Thus, the essence of my teaching is
perceive the simple connectedness of all life
realize one's true consciousness
reduce Self interest-ego
and lessen the pull of the senses and a busy mind

19

Smartness and intellectualism are mostly a function of memory stored in the brain. Again and again Lao Tzu expressed the preference for the use of the whole mind instead of relying too much on the brain.

Intellectualism is a function of memories stored in the brain. The brain, being a physical organ is temporary as are the memories stored in the brain. At the end of a lifetime the brain deteriorates as do the memories stored there. The mind, however, is engaged anytime we make choices and exercise the imagination.

Since thought is the cause of all creation the more we upgrade our thoughts with choice to think new thoughts of a more lofty nature, the more we increase the opportunity to progress on the ladder of soul evolution.

Justice and morality are needed to teach human thinking people to exist with each other peacefully yet it is enforced externally. Obedience to the inner soul urging for growth and enlightenment and devotion to that ideal are of a higher nature than any physical rules of order.

Cleverness is a function of the brain. Profit is based upon getting ahead in physical life. Neither usually addresses the inner Self. Waste, greed, and theft are based upon physical thinking. They are not grounded in the mental, Universal Laws of Creation. There are many smart people in the world. There are fewer wise people.

Lao Tzu even states that these three remedies treat outward, physical forms and physical life only. Therefore, to live the higher and greater life based on higher ideals is important and essential. It is absolutely essential to discipline the mind in order to raise consciousness to know the truth of the connectedness of all creation and that each person is an immortal I AM.

Jesus of Nazareth named two commandments as the greatest. 1. Thou shalt Love your God with all your Heart and all your soul and all your mind and 2. you shall love your neighbor as yourself. Jesus names Love as greater than anything else that one can do or be. All goodness is contained in love. Kindness is contained in love. All quickened soul growth through greater connectedness is in love. Jesus said, *"Why store up treasures where thieves can steal and rust can corrode, where moths can eat."* Only that which is temporary and therefore relates to form can be stolen or destroyed. That which is eternal can never be stolen or destroyed.

Outward forms are not sufficient because in themselves, they are temporary. It is more important to have and know the still and quiet mind. The still and quiet conscious mind can be aligned with subconscious mind and the two attuned to Superconscious mind. It is in Superconscious Mind that oneness or union with all creation and creator is achieved, known and realized.

To know this oneness one must first have let go of all selfishness. Selfishness is based upon a false conception that self is alone, separate, disconnected and disjointed from all creation and from every other person in creation.

To live life from an understanding of connectedness gives one power over selfishness and power over the physical desire to possess forms. These limiting and temporary forms are replaced by the immortal Self and eternal life of expanded consciousness that is full of LIGHT, Truth and Love. Physical possessions and physical desires are temporary.

Each soul while living in a physical body needs to come to progressively master their individual mind and the whole of Universal Mind in order to know Self as a permanent and lasting offspring of the Creator and one with all Creation.

The lesson is:
You can try to create the perfect outer environment in which to learn. More important, is to create a productive attitude of consciousness. This is the great learning.

Twenty

A definite reply of yes in contrast to a hesitant
      reply of yeah has little difference
Good and bad how much alike or different are they
The one who creates fear, lives in fear,
why should I fear what others fear
The wild, undisciplined mind will never bring an
      end to this
The masses are stimulated and excited as if
      celebrating a great feast
As in spring some take part in the feast in the park and
climb the lookout platform
I alone have a still mind and am without
      engrossing desires
Like a baby who has not yet smiled
I am alone without others of like mind
Others have more than they need
I alone appear to be left out and possess nothing
My mind is foolish and simple
others try to look bright and intelligent
while I seem dim and confused
Common people are smart
I seem to be dull and withdrawn
I resemble a calm ocean
I appear to be anchored and without a destination
Everyone else is engaged in their busy activity
Yet I, the knower of the Tao
appear to be stubborn and lowly
I, a knower of the Tao, differ from the people
For I am nourished by the Great Mother

20

Yes and no, beautiful and ugly, are functions of pairs of opposites, the Maya or illusion of the physical life and sensory experiences. Learn to recognize similarities like yes and yeah. Learn to recognize what seems to be opposites.

The one with an undisciplined mind lives mostly in the brain with memory thoughts of separation. This is a false perception of reality that leads to fear.

The disciplined mind is a still mind. The still mind is receptive and absorbs learning like a child or baby. In the disciplined mind the pairs of opposites, the Maya of illusion, is replaced by the awareness of the Aggressive and Receptive Principles of Creation of Superconscious Mind.

For such a one the mind is simple. It is outward, physical life that makes things complicated. A still mind receives all learning and comes to know Self and all creation. Brain learning is physical memorization of facts.

As long as life is viewed from a physical perspective, so long will life seem complicated. Viewing life from a physical way is to see life as complicated because everything is perceived to be separate and disjointed. This illusion of separateness is a factor of the limitations of the five physical senses which is the structure or vehicle used by the conscious mind to perceive in the physical environment.

Still the mind. Align the inner and outer minds and life becomes understandable because the cause of each thing and event can be comprehended. The interconnectedness of all things is known. Judgement keeps one entrapped in the physical body. Judgement keeps one entrapped in the pairs of opposites that are easily perceivable in the physical world. Yes and no, good and evil, are forms of the pairs of opposites. These pairs of opposites are limiting forms or reflections of the Aggressive and Receptive Principles of Superconscious Mind. These aggressive and receptive principles are known in China as Yin and Yang. The I Ching refers to these as the Yin and Yang.

These two are the principles of continual creation. They are available for the soul to use for continual learning and growth. The one who falls under the power of the pairs of opposites practices avoidance. Avoidance of learning, growth and continual creation.

The one who thinks physically and lives physically while ignoring the inner urge goes through life sometimes contented, sometimes fearful. The one with a strong inner urge to know the Self and all creation fearlessly leaves behind the old ways of fear. Such a one is not content with the limitations of the parents or others in the environment. Such a one must find the answers to the mysteries of life and make those truths a complete manifestation within the Self.

The statement "I alone appear to be left out and possess nothing" is like the statement by Jesus, *"The birds have their nests and the foxes their lairs, but the Son of Man has nowhere to lay his head."*

The inner urge to know, to become enlightened, to reach a state of connectedness is strong in the one who has built many permanent and eternal understandings of creation in past lives. A highly evolved soul has enough Self awareness to know that something is not right with the way life is and the manner in which others are experiencing life.

A highly evolved soul knows even while still a child, that he is different from those around the Self. Such youth notice they are different from others and wonders why. They know the world is not quite right, that something is wrong. Without knowing what it is, they often erroneously think something is wrong with the Self.

Even though such a one feels the Self to be alone because he or she is different still one has an inner drive and an inner nourishment that comes by being so strongly and consciously connected to the Real Self, the inner Self.

The Great Mother is nature, the living physical world which is connected to the inner, mental spiritual world. Such a one loves trees, planting trees, growing trees, learning from trees. Such an enlightened soul loves plants, loves gardens and loves to teach others the inner secrets of plants.

Such an enlightened soul knows the earth to be alive and is in tune with the living Earth Mother. This one is connected in Love to all the earth, all the plants and trees of the earth, and all living things. Such a being is one with the Mother Earth through Love.

The lesson is:

To still the mind and receive the learning in every experience. The greatest desire is the need to know the Self.

Twenty-one

The greatest power is developed in those who
       follow the Tao completely
The Tao is elusive and formless
elusive and formless yet within it is an image
elusive and formless yet within is structure
within it is the spirit, the essence, the life force
       of all things
this essence is hidden yet real
within it resides universal truth from
       the most ancient of times

From the beginning of Creation to the present
its name has never changed
In order that we might discern the vibration of
       Creation
How do I know the vibration of Creation?
Through this
the very vibration that is sounding right now
is within me

The Tao is LIGHT vibration and Life Force that manifests through the plan of creation held in Superconscious Mind. The Superconscious Mind is intangible and elusive because it is not physical. It is beyond the physical world and universe.

The Superconscious Mind holds the plan of creation and the life force to accomplish this plan. This life force from Superconscious Mind is the essence or core of the entire Subconscious and Conscious Mind. The seed idea or plan and the energy to make manifest that plan is the essence of everything experienced in the physical environment. Thus, the greatest power is to harmonize with the Tao, the LIGHT of Creation for we also are beings of LIGHT.

The image referred to is the seed idea or plan held in Superconscious Mind. The Superconscious Mind is intangible and elusive because it operates at a higher rate of vibration than physical matter. Therefore, the five physical senses cannot perceive the Superconscious Mind. The five physical senses can only perceive the physical environment. They perceive physical objects, physical form, and physical substance.

The Superconscious Mind is elusive and formless yet within is structure because the perfect seed idea or plan is the structure of creation and forms the framework for all of Mind. Each individual uses it in order to advance in awareness. In a similar fashion a blueprint for a house is a form or seed idea or plan for what will become a physical house.

This essence, this plan, this seed idea held in Superconscious Mind is very real, for without it people could not even exist in physical bodies in the physical environment. The Superconscious Mind supplies the life force to the physical life. This is why Jesus, who became a Christ, said, *"It is written that it is not by bread alone that man can live but by every word which proceeds from the mouth of God"* (Matthew 4:4).

Since the essence called Superconscious Mind is very real yet not perceivable by the five senses the intuitive thinker must listen to the inner urge of the soul. This is called stilling the mind and listening to the truth that is universal and comes from the inner Self.

This perfect plan, this perfect seed idea or blueprint was the beginning of manifestation of all life experiences in form. This plan continues to exist. It can be known by those who learn to still the mind and listen to the inner Self.

The vibration of Creation is AUM. Know the plan and you will know creation. How can one come to know the vibration of creation and follow it? The answer is to still the mind and hear the vibration of Creation. In order to harmonize with the vibration of Creation sound the AUM vibration.

The lesson is:

Go deep into meditation to know
the structure of mind and creation.
Sound the aum to harmonize with creation.
Still the mind in order to perceive – hear
the vibration of creation.

Twenty-two

Yield and become complete
Bend and become straightened
Empty and become full
Wear out and be renewed
Have little and gain much
Have much and be confused

Therefore, the Sage embraces the One unity
and thus becomes an example to the world
not showing off he shines forth
not promoting himself he is distinguished
not boasting he gains continual merit
not being conceited his greatness leads

Because he does not compete
no one can compete against him
The ancients who said yield and become complete
were not just saying empty words
Becoming whole and complete depends on
yielding

One who yields or bends is flexible. One who is flexible can adapt to changing conditions. The nature of physical life is change because physical life is temporary. By being flexible, changing, and adapting, one can learn to master the Self thus gaining control within Self which in turn gives one power to create.

A young sapling that twists or bends in the wind can become straight again when the wind ceases to blow. The large or old tree that is not so flexible breaks in a strong wind and cannot grow straight as it did before.

When you give of yourself freely the Self is constantly renewed. *"As you give so you shall receive,"* says the Bible.

The one who receives gains more because such a one keeps the energy of Self and creation in motion. Stopping or retarding the energy of giving stops the energy of receiving. The entire Universe operates in cycles. Giving and receiving is a cycle.

As one teaches what has been learned, the Self opens a place inside the soul to gain greater learning of the Laws of Creation.

One who uses something completely has the opportunity to use that energy completely, to the fullest and thus, begin a new cycle of learning. The key to success and creation in this regard is to always produce more than one consumes. This is the hallmark of a mental adult, which is one who is living and applying reasoning in the life. The thinker creates a greater stage of learning before the present opportunity is complete.

The one who has little has less possessions to which to be attached. This is the meaning of the phrase, *"Have little and gain much."* Attachments create misery says Gautama the Buddha, in the Dhammapada 5:75, *"Choose the path that leads to Nirvana: avoid the road to profit and pleasure. Remember this always, O disciples of the Buddha, and strive always for wisdom."*

Attachment to desires brings misery. One who has many possessions may find the mind is always dwelling on those possessions and the desire for more possessions. This keeps the person engrossed in the physical life, entrapped in a physical body and falsely enamored with the physical world, the world of Maya. Maya is the illusion that the physical world is all there is to life and creation and that everything is separate and disconnected. One is under the power of Maya, of illusion when the Self is engrossed in the five physical senses allowing them to control the Self.

To embrace the One Unity is to realize you are, I AM. It is to accept your inner divinity as an individual. It is to admit and realize you are more than a physical body. In fact, you are not a temporary physical body at all. You are an eternal soul inhabiting a physical body for the purpose of developing in soul growth and learning to apply the Laws of Creation in order to know Self as I AM, a being of LIGHT. It is to accept the truth that everything and everyone is connected.

A great LIGHT of awareness shines forth from such a one who exists as an I AM full of LIGHT and understanding. There is no need to pretend to be something else which is to be something less.

A person centered in the Real Self keeps the attention on learning and growth, giving and receiving love, and the freedom of the movement of LIGHT filled energy. Such a one does not need to brag or prove anything for the enlightened being knows and is a knower and is secure in the knowing.

For a knower there is no need for debate; therefore, no need to quarrel.

The greatest return on investment for an advanced soul is the permanent understandings or lessons of life gained from each experience. To gain the soul lesson is more important than receiving a physical object.

To compete against someone or something is to direct the attention outward into the physical environment in an attempt to gain a temporary, false sense of security.

When one no longer competes then the attention is freed and can be placed fully on receiving the learning that adds to the whole Self. Therefore, whatever the lesson, be flexible enough to receive it. Receive the Higher Truth into the Self. Becoming a whole functioning Self does depend upon surrendering or yielding one's conscious ego that views the Self and the world as separate and apart from Self.

All the Universe and all of Mind is connected. Whatever you do to another you also do unto Self. This is why Jesus the Christ said, *"Whatever you wish men to do for you, do likewise also for them; for this is the law and the Prophets," (Matthew 7:12).*

The lesson is:

Be flexible and willing to change. Surrender the conscious ego and be connected.

Twenty-three

To speak only when needed is the natural way
strong wind does not last the whole morning
Rain storms do not last the whole day
Heaven and Earth create these events
If Heaven and Earth cannot make things last long
how much less so the work of man

Therefore,
one who is committed to the Way
identifies with the Way
one who is committed to success
identifies with success
one who is committed to failure
identifies with failure

to the one who thinks about success
the Way gives success
to the one who thinks about failure
the Way gives failure

The five physical senses are sense receptors. This means the five senses receive impressions from the physical environment. It is through receiving that a person learns.

When one stops talking one can listen. When one stills the chattering mind one can receive. All great spiritual teachers understand the power of receptivity. Rain storms symbolize the confusion in the conscious mind that occurs when the thoughts in the mind are allowed to race. The enlightened being stills the Mind and is in tune with the Superconscious Mind and the vibration of Creation, which is AUM.

He who stills the mind and listens to the inner urge to know, to be enlightened comes to know the Perfect Plan for Creation held in Superconscious Mind. Such a one comes to know I AM and is one with the Tao. A still mind is a good and productive mind. Every time you speak you have first created a thought in the conscious mind. To create a thought is to disrupt a still mind. Therefore, be committed to becoming an en-LIGHT-ened being, a Christ, a Lao Tzu, a Buddha. Let greater enlightenment be your success. Do not accept failure in this because failure is not one's inherent nature. It is the duty of Self to gain enlightenment.

All things of our physical life are temporary. This is the point of the first six verses. If Heaven and Earth cannot make strong wind and rain storms last very long then why should we think our physical actions and physical works will last long or endure? What will endure is the soul learning brought to and integrated into the Self in a lifetime. What will endure is the soul learning and wisdom that is taught to others.

Thought is the cause of our lives and of all creation. There-fore, think thoughts of success. *"Union of all parts of mind (yoga) is gained through the control of the action of the mind,"* says The Yogi Sutras of Patanjali, Book 1, Sutra 2.

The lesson is:

***Always have an open, disciplined mind
that can achieve stillness.
When a thought is chosen,
let it be of the success of enlightenment.***

***Cause enlightened thoughts to manifest in our physical
world as a greater consciousness for all.***

Twenty-four

One who stands on tiptoes is not steady
one who straddles the fence cannot walk far
one who pretends outwardly is not enlightened
one who asserts self forcefully has little value
one who praises self does not achieve
      permanence

From the perspective of the Tao
we may call these:
excess food and unneeded baggage
these things do not bring happiness

Therefore,
the one in harmony with the Way
does not indulge in them

24

Each day is a new opportunity to grow and add to one's vibrational quickening. The steps on the ladder of soul growth must be accomplished every day. One goes from the first floor of a house to the second floor by climbing steps. One moves and expands the consciousness from the physical or Conscious Mind to Subconscious Mind to Superconscious Mind in steps. This series of unceasing steps upward is accomplished by utilizing the power of the will and the power of the imaging capability or imagination.

The one who stands on tiptoes is attempting to temporarily perceive higher or accomplish more. The one who straddles the fence finds forward progress difficult because there is a need to make a decision, to move one way or the other. However, it is the continual process of forward motion of consciousness, which is the process of adding to one's awareness and understanding that produces sustained and immortal results. Seek a permanent higher consciousness. To make a show, to pretend outwardly, to boast, to brag is to have one's consciousness engrossed in and controlled by outer situations, circumstances, and stimuli. This will not endure and is temporary.

This excess food called information fails to satisfy, for it does not nourish the soul. The unneeded baggage of emotional attachments weighs self down. They are the encumbrances of attachment to physical desires. This keeps the attention on physical things and objects of temporary desire instead of on the eternal.

Those things that are temporary do not bring happiness. The soul learning that builds permanent understanding brings lasting fulfillment, LIGHT, truth, Love and connectedness.

Those who choose to quicken their LIGHT vibration and movement to enlightenment avoid getting bogged down in physical desires and emotional attachments.

Those who listen and follow their inner urge to fulfill the plan of Creation called the Way or the Tao fulfill their Holy Assignment. They refuse engrossment in the sensory experiences. They gain Enlightenment. They exist as LIGHT with conscious awareness and understanding of Self as I AM, an individualized being of LIGHT.

The lesson is:

*All action and all thought
is to be used for the advancement
of the soul.*

Everything else is temporary.

Twenty-five

There was something formless and complete
that was before Heaven and Earth
vast and still, unchanging and standing alone
it stands on its own and is everywhere
it may be considered as the Mother of Heaven and
Earth
not yet knowing its name
I call it the Tao
forced to name it further
I would call it, The Great
The Great that flows ever forward
an ever flowing that functions everywhere and is far
reaching
I would further describe this far reaching
as returning to the place of origin

The Tao is great
Heaven is great
Earth is great
the highest aspect of Man is also great
In the universe there are four greats
and Man the thinker is one among them
Man patterns himself on the Earth
the Earth patterns itself on Heaven
Heaven patterns itself on the Tao
The Tao patterns itself on its own nature

Before people were created, before Earth was formed, before Mind was created, LIGHT was created as an expression or movement outward of the creative thought of the Creator. This all pervasive LIGHT is the LIGHT of awareness from the Creator.

This is explained and presented in the Bible, *Book of John,* Chapter 1, Verse 1, King James: *"In the beginning was the Word and the Word was with God and the Word was God."* or Lamsa: 1. *"The Word was in the beginning, and that very Word was with God, and God was that Word."* 2. *"The same was in the beginning with God."*

The word is the Tao. In order to form and say a word a creator must have a thought. The word is used to describe the thought. The thought of the creator that was and is described by the word of the Creator is the Perfect Plan or Seed Idea of Creation.

This creation has been going on and moving forward since the original expression or outpouring of the Creator's creative impulse. This was the beginning of physical time. Physical time and creation have been moving forward ever since.

The Creator's LIGHT, which is the LIGHT of awareness, and the Creator's Word which is the movement toward fulfillment of the Plan of Creation has been ever present and in motion ever since that initial outpouring.

The Tao is called the Great, because the Plan of Creation and the movement of LIGHT forward in creation is the great source of our life, experience, and awareness. LIGHT is ever returning because the energies of creation are continuously recycling through all of Mind.

Heaven, which symbolizes Superconscious Mind, is also great for Heaven contains the Divine Plan for our Creation.

Earth is great for Earth symbolizes Subconscious, Universal Mind. It is the abode of the soul. The word man which comes from the Sanskrit word Manu means thinker. A thinker existing in a physical body patterns the Self on the soul existing in Subconscious Mind.

Superconscious Mind patterns itself on LIGHT. LIGHT patterns itself on its own Nature.

The lesson is:

Harmonize conscious and subconscious minds of Self and attune them to Superconscious Mind and live in LIGHT while becoming en-LIGHT-ened.

Twenty-six

The temporary inner is the foundation
     of the temporary outer
Stillness is the master of restless

Therefore, the Sage may travel all day
without getting far from his important treasure
though there may be gorgeous sights to see
he stays calm and unattached

What does this mean
How then should a Lord with ten thousand chariots
take himself too lightly before all under Heaven
To seek one's treasure in the temporary outer
is to be separated from one's foundation
To have a busy or restless mind is to
lose command

LIGHT moves outward first through Superconscious Mind then to Subconscious Mind and then to the Conscious Mind which we call our physical world and Universe. This is why the inner is the foundation of the outer.

The movement outward through the divisions of Mind is a process whereby the vibration of Creation slows down becoming more dense or heavy. Frozen cosmic energy which is called physical matter and form is heavy. It is the root of LIGHT in that it is the farthest movement outward or downward from LIGHT just as a tree has its most downward part in the root system.

All thought begins in the Mind. Thought is a motion in mind. When the mind is brought under the control of the thinker and the restless thoughts disappear the Self experiences a still mind. The mind is still and the person experiences peace. Then the thinker, the disciplined individual is free to choose a thought that will move the Self forward into a more expansive consciousness. Thus, a still mind is able to rule the motion of the mind.

The real and important treasure is what is permanent and lasting. The thinker does not allow Self to be ensnared and engrossed in temporary sensory gratification of desire fulfillment. Being calm the thinker has a still mind. Having a still mind sensory stimuli from the physical environment do not have control. Such a one is the master of his own destiny and the quickness with which it is achieved.

The Lord of 10,000 chariots is the I AM or thinker who has mastered the thousands of aspects of Self. Such a one can direct all aspects of Self in a powerful manner toward the fulfillment of the ultimate destiny of enlightenment.

To be light is to gain en-LIGHT-enment. Then the root of physical engrossment in sensory stimuli and the illusion it provides is overcome. The root of desire that binds the Self to the physical plane is released and overcome. The Self is free to soar in all levels of mind.

The still mind gives one control of Self, mind, and the quickening of one's soul growth and Spiritual evolution.

The lesson is:

Still the mind
and perceive the world as it is in reality.
Value the Real inner Self.

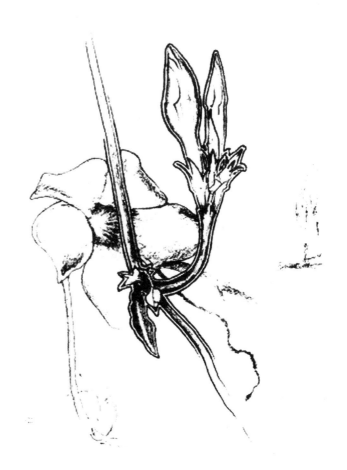

Twenty-seven

The skilled traveler leaves no tracks
the skilled speaker reveals no flaws
the skilled counter uses no tally beads
the skilled closer locks no locks
      yet what he closes cannot be opened
the one skilled at binding uses neither rope or cord
      yet what he binds cannot be untied
for these reasons
    the Sage is always excellent at saving others
    and does not abandon them
    the Sage is always excellent at taking care of
    all things
without any waste
This is called useful enlightenment

Therefore,
The good man is the teacher for the good
and the bad man is the lesson for the good man
to not value and appreciate one's teacher
and not love one's lessons
even though one has knowledge is delusion
This is called the essence of truth

Tracks are a temporary sign of one's movement in the sensory, physical world.

A skilled speaker uses the Universal Language of Mind which is the language of pictures. One who learns to describe accurately with words the mental thoughts held in the mind is a good speaker for the mental image is communicated effectively.

A skilled counter is one who forms complete, lasting mental images. These lasting mental images may be drawn forth as memory, at any time. Thus individual parts are drawn together into a comprehensive whole.

The physical world is temporary. Superconscious Mind is permanent and lasting. The enlightened being opens the door and closes the door to the inner levels of mind by choice and will.

Only the will and imaging faculty of the thinker can open and close this door to the whole mind and Christ consciousness.

Skilled binding requires no knots because the Universal Principles of Love and Truth that bind or connect one individual to another form a continuous, unbroken stream of consciousness between these beings. No one can loosen the knots of Love. No one can destroy Truth. Truth and Love are eternal. They are one with the immortal.

The Sage, the enlightened one recognizes and realizes with all people, all life, and all creation there is the inner urge to aid and help all. His kindness and love abounds. The thinker knows that as one aids others in their soul growth and spiritual development the Self becomes more and more like the Creator which is to have universal or cosmic consciousness.

All beings must be raised up in consciousness. Therefore, the enlightened become world teachers raising the consciousness of all mankind.

This is called following the LIGHT and leading others to the LIGHT and enlightenment.

The word man means thinker. What is a productive thinker? One who uplifts the consciousness of others. Those who have yet to rise out of the limitations of entrapment need a spiritual teacher to lead them out of their limitations.

All of creation, all rapid soul growth, all quickening is based upon the student-teacher relationship and upon being willing to learn the lessons that life affords.

When the teacher is not respected no one learns and no one grows in soul consciousness. Those who desire to accelerate their soul growth need a teacher of Mind. There must always be love between teacher and student.

The teacher-student connectedness is vital to their growth of the individual, society, and civilization. This is the explanation of the mystery. One can learn the fastest from one who knows, when one is willing.

The lesson is:

*To be open minded
and willing to receive from all in one's
environment especially one's teacher
and those with more experience.*

Twenty-eight

Know the aggressive quality of the male
while maintaining the receptive quality of the female
be the receptive, feminine principle, the maid
being the receptive, feminine principle, the maid of the world
your permanent power will not depart
when your permanent power does not depart
you will achieve the qualities of infancy

Know the bright
be determined when encountering darkness
and you will be an example for the world
Being an example for the world
permanent power is fulfilled
when permanent power is fulfilled
you will achieve the infinite expansion of consciousness

Know the glory
hold firm to the humility
and be a model for the world
Being a model for the world
you will maintain commitment to eternal truth
by maintaining commitment to eternal truth
you will gain expansion of consciousness with no
limitations

When the block of wood is sawed up
it becomes useful
when the Sage is used
he becomes the director of leaders
because great carving is accomplished
without splitting things into pieces

In order for any creation to occur there needs to exist both the aggressive and receptive principles within that creation.

To be the maid of the world is to always be open to receive the learning in every experience. To be the maid of the world is to be receptive and draw all experiences needed by the soul to the Self.

To be directed is to apply the aggressive quality in the life to cause forward motion that will cause higher states of consciousness and permanent power.

To be directed with power is to make choices that improve the Self and lift one's thoughts and consciousness to a greater alignment with Universal Law and Universal Truth.

Thus, one obtains the quality of infancy which is the ability to absorb all learning, knowledge, information, and experience into the Self.

Pure learning of Self and creation, to know the whole Mind and to align with the Universal Laws and Truths, are the desires and needs of all souls who are diligently striving to gain enlightenment.

One who teaches others to know Self and gain greater enlightenment is a receptively productive example. A Master teacher is receptive to the students and is committed to their soul growth.

The individual who gives the highest service by teaching the learning that has been gained through discipline of the mind is the one who achieves the infinite expansion of consciousness which is the Christ Consciousness.

Brightness comes from light. The glory of White Light is that it is a combination of all the colors of the light spectrum. White, being a combination of all colors reflects the light that is received. This is why on hot days one wears white clothes in order to be cool.

In the darkness one experiences black. Black absorbs light. This is why people do not wear black clothes in hot sun.

Black and white are opposites as are hot and cold. *Revelation 3:14-16* says, *"And to the angel of the church in Laodicea write: 'These things says the Amen, the faithful and true witness, the beginning of the Creation of God. I know your words, that you are neither cold nor hot; it is better to be either cold or hot. So then because you are lukewarm, and neither cold nor hot, I will spew you out of my mouth'."*

Hot and cold symbolize the Yin and Yang, the Aggressive and Receptive Principles of Creation. A thinker, a creator is sometimes aggressive, sometimes receptive, never confusing the two and never becoming entrapped in the pairs of opposites.

The sun gives light, and black outer space receives the Light. In physical life black is receptive and receives light while white is aggressive and gives light. Thus, the one who gains a balance and understanding of both is a model for the world. Such a one has achieved permanent commitment to know Self and to aid all humanity. Black relates to humility and Light relates to glory.

All resources are for our use. The proper use is to cause learning and growth that adds to one's soul understandings.

Carving wood is used as an analogy for molding and shaping our life and experiences. Great carving is accomplished without splitting things up because the true nature of creation and all of mind is connectedness. To split things up is to view the world under the illusion of separateness, or Maya.

The lesson is:

Use the aggressive and receptive principles of creation. Become a master at using these two great principles and cause greater connectedness within Self and on planet Earth.

Twenty-nine

Concerning those who desire to control the world with
force
I perceive they cannot succeed
All that is under Heaven is a sacred vessel
it is not something that can be controlled
those who control it will ruin it
those who try to control it will lose it

Therefore, concerning beings
some times one leads, other times one follows
some times one breathes out, other times one breathes
in
some times one is strong, other times one is weak

Therefore the Sage
        avoids extremes
        avoids excess
        avoids extravagance

29

To try to control the world is to think of Self as separate from the world. This is wrong thinking. We are connected with everything and everyone else.

This verse is a continuation of the thought of Chapter 28, namely the productive use of the Aggressive and Receptive Principles of Creation.

The true nature of reality is connectedness. Therefore, just as the physical body is a sacred vessel or vehicle for the soul so is every other soul's physical body a sacred vessel. All are connected in LIGHT. What is done to another is also first done to the Self. We are designed to be creators not controllers. *Genesis* 1:2 says: *"Let us make man in our image, after our likeness." Genesis* 1:27 says; *"God created man in his own image, in the image of God he created him; male and female he created them."*

Therefore, it is our duty to create as our Creator creates through free choice and imagination.

Image = imagination

Cold and hot are opposite extremes. To lead or follow are opposites. To be silent or talk a lot are opposites. To be strong or weak are opposites.

By avoiding extremes the Self does not fall under the power of the pairs of opposites which is the illusion that the physical life and all life is separate. When life is seen as connected, extremes are reduced and eliminated.

Excess and extravagance are extremes. Causing oneself to have a still mind eliminates extremes. A still and quiet mind is the beginning of knowing the connectedness and oneness of all creation.

With the still and quiet mind the enlightened thinker causes continual forward motion leading to the expansion of a balanced consciousness and the fulfillment of Self as a being of LIGHT.

To gain mastery of Mind one must gain harmony within the Self and with others. One needs to build this connectedness into an unbroken stream of unity consciousness.

The lesson is:

Still the mind.
Move and work in harmony with creation,
with others, and with nature. Harmonize
with your environment.
Lead when needed. Follow when needed.

Thirty

One who assists the ruler in the way of the Tao
counsels him not to use force against all under Heaven
such effort is certain to bring about retaliation
where armies are stationed
thorns and thistles grow

A good thinker achieves his goal and that is all
he uses power but does not make use of force
in the same way
achieve your goal but do not become arrogant
achieve your goal but do not praise your deeds
achieve your goal but do not brag
achieve your goal and win when you have no choice
this is called achieving one's goal without using force

Those who achieve through force may flourish for a while then
fade away
what is not in harmony with the Tao comes to an early end
Force is not in harmony with the Tao

The way of the Tao – the way LIGHT uses the Perfect Plan of Creation held in Superconscious Mind – is to use the Aggressive and Receptive Principles of Creation in balance. The Aggressive and Receptive Principles of Creation are named Yang and Yin.

Force and taking are the destructive misuse of the aggressive and receptive principles. Therefore, there is resistance. Therefore, all gains are temporary.

To do what needs to be done is to respond. This is responsibility. Responsibility is the hallmark of a thinker, a learned being. Power is creating. Force is destroying. Always create. Adding to, building upon, and improving what is in one's environment and in the Self is also the hallmark of a thinker.

To achieve results is to move forward in one's consciousness and to continually build and add to what already exists in the environment.

Do not feed the conscious ego with false illusions of grandeur. These are distractions that keep one limited, engrossed, and entrapped in physical life and the physical body.

The natural way is to create and add to what is in your environment. The natural, organic way is to work with others to create a better world and a more enlightened Self.

Violence destroys. Love, goodness, truth and LIGHT create. Be a creator. Therefore help others. Love others. Teach others and give service to others.

A goal gives the mind direction. A purpose gives the Self motivation and a personal benefit.

To have as a purpose the idea of impressing others is an external purpose and is therefore weak. A strong purpose benefits the Self permanently. Therefore, a strong purpose will always add to one's learning and growth and will make one a better person.

A weak purpose is temporary for it depends on whether or not one can receive a response or reaction from another.

The goal and purpose is not meant to out do another person. The goal is meant to give the mind direction for the purpose of adding to one's soul growth and the fulfillment of permanent understanding of Self, and mind. This permanent understanding is then stored in subconscious mind which is the soul of Self.

Whatever is sent forth from Self be it mental, emotional or physical will return to Self in like manner. Therefore, force is followed by loss of strength. For force is the misuse of energy to overpower another.

The way of the Tao is complete harmonization. Love is harmony. The way of the Tao is love. Love connects. The way of the Tao is connectedness. The way of force is to separate and alienate.

That which fails to unite, build, and create is temporary. That which unites souls in bonds of Divine Love, Light and Truth is permanent, lasting and eternal.

The Tao Te Ching devotes several chapters in a row to the subject of power, control and force. The solution to all of these is given as harmony.

The lesson is:

Give the mind direction.
Cooperate and harmonize with others for
mutual quickening of awareness and understanding.
Seek to create and be in harmony
in all that is accomplished.
Eternal youth is
eternally adding to what is already present.

Thirty-one

Concerning weapons
they are instruments of unproductive omen
Creation and all creatures are against them
Therefore,

> One who harmonizes with the Tao
> does not use them

The ruler who is wise in ordinary life
prefers the left the side of rest
When at war the ruler prefers the right, the side of action
weapons are not the instrument of a reasoner
weapons are instruments of fear
to be used only when there is no choice
The superior man cherishes the peace of a still mind
and never looks upon weapons as objects of beauty
to think weapons are beautiful
is to delight in the killing of others
one who enjoys the killing of people
will never realize the goal of fulfillment in the world
It is because of this that:
On happy events we appreciate the left
on occasions for mourning the greatest honor
is given to the right
Therefore,

> A minister stands on the left
> and the supreme general stands on the right

The point is:

> They arrange themselves as they would at a funeral
> When many people are killed
> they should be mourned in heartfelt sorrow
> That is why the victory in battle
> is to be treated like a funeral ceremony

Weapons destroy. All intelligent and wise people, all thinkers, all who wish to fulfill the Dharma, all who love, all builders, all who are connected, create. They do not destroy. Weapons are instruments of destruction.

Followers of the Tao create. The Tao is the Perfect Plan of Creation held in Superconscious Mind and the life force that fulfills it. Destruction is against the Creator.

The left is the power of receptivity and the power to surrender the ego and align the consciousness with connectedness. The right is the side of aggressiveness that can be misused as force.

The wise person always prefers peace. The quiet and still mind leads to an open heart. An open heart allows love to be released in the Self as one is transformed.

Overpowering another is not a reason for rejoicing or happiness. Rather, it is a time of sadness that peace and connectedness was not maintained.

To delight in killing is to enjoy destroying. To enjoy destroying is to remove all opportunities for the quickening of one's evolution and growth into an energy body.

On happy occasions people are open and receptive. They share love and LIGHT. During destructive times people are closed off from fear of hurt and pain.

When opportunities for learning and growth are destroyed sorrow ensues. There is no victory through force only a temporary false sense of control.

The subject of force, control and power from earlier chapters is continued here with the addition of the factor of weapons. In physical life weapons are usually used to kill people and therefore rob them of the opportunity in a physical incarnation of building soul growth and spiritual development.

Using the Universal Language of Mind, the same language used in dream interpretation, weapons symbolize tools of change.

Death in a dream symbolizes change. Yet to kill or be killed in a dream is to change without being in control.

Violence is a result of the thoughts of Self being out of control. Violence occurs from thinking physical instead of in a mental way and from forgetting who you are as a soul and as an eternal I AM.

The goal of fulfillment in creation is to learn to be a creator. To kill is to take away learning opportunities.

Physical victory over others is to be mourned for it only reduces opportunities for soul growth and spiritual development. The Buddha says in the Dhammapada 3:42, *"More than those who hate you, more than all your enemies, an undisciplined mind does greater harm. More than your mother, more than your father, more than all your family, a well-disciplined mind does greater good."*

The lesson is:

*Learn to discipline the mind
in order to use the opportunities of life to the fullest.
Create and learn in and through the creations of Self
and others.*

*Learn with a still mind
and an open heart. Always discipline the mind.
Gain control of one's thoughts. Choose thoughts
carefully and with diligence.*

Thirty-two

The Tao (Way) is eternally nameless
Even though in its simplicity it seems insignificant
no one in the world can master it
If Kings and feudal Lords could live in accordance
with it
everything in the world would submit of their
own accord
Heaven and Earth would align in harmony
to send forth sweet dew
This gently rain of dew would fall equally on all
causing the people to live in harmony
without being ordered to do so

As soon as the whole is divided into parts
there are names to describe the separation
Once there are names given
then one must know when to stop separating
in order to identify
By knowing when to stop one will come to no harm

The similarity of all under heaven to the Way
is like the relationship of valley streams and
rivers that flow to the ocean

The Tao which is the perfect plan of Creation held in Superconscious Mind and the life force to accomplish this task is not observable by the five senses. Yet it pervades and is at the essence and core of everything.

All the power of the universe is available to the person who aligns with this Perfect Plan of Creation. To align with this Perfect Plan of Creation one must exist in and practice light, love and truth. For love connects. Love unifies. Love draws together. It is only through connectedness which leads to oneness that the power of the universe can be made available to an individual. An individual must be connected to the universe in order to use the power of the universe.

When the Perfect Plan of Creation is followed all learning, soul growth, and Spiritual development proceed rapidly. There is a quickening of the inner movement and motion of the Self.

For the physically engrossed, the physical life of matter seems to consist of a group of separate parts. When objects, things, and people are seen to be separate, one lacks power. Trying to identify all the parts will not give one mastery of the Self or the Whole Mind.

To know when to stop is to still the mind and gain peace. Then one can become connected to the universe. To flow is harmony. To flow in the same direction as the plan of creation allows one to experience the ocean of consciousness and its power.

The brain and five senses of sight, smell, taste, touch and hearing attempt constantly to separate out and identify one object from another. Too much separating and identifying keeps one from admitting one's part in the scheme of things which becomes an obstruction to knowing the connectedness of Self and all creation.

Four steps for gaining greater awareness and understanding for the conscious mind and for knowing the inner subconscious mind of Self are:

1. **Separate**
2. **Identify**
3. **Admit**
4. **Connect**

Most physical sciences use the qualities of separate and identify. These two work mostly with the brain and five senses. Logic is a function mostly of the brain.

To admit, which is number 3, is to understand your part in things and your effect and influence on the whole. The fourth part or stage is to then connect to a great degree with the whole Self, the environment, and the universe.

To separate into parts is to exist in the conscious mind and brain. This leads to confusion.

To use the mind to perceive the connectedness of all things, and all beings is to know the similarity of all beings and simplicity of the Mind.

Each individual, each I AM, is connected to the Creator and creation like streams and rivers to the ocean.

The lesson is:

To separate and identify everything is important for the building up of reasoning.

To admit one's part in creation is power. To connect is absolutely essential for enlightenment.

Thirty-three

Understanding others is intelligent
understanding Self is Enlightenment
conquering others is force
conquering Self is power
Knowing what is enough is wealth
Going forward with determination is will power
To be aware of your center is to live long
To die but not be forgotten is continuous life

To achieve the stage of growth known as wisdom requires that one teach. There are four stages of growth. They are infancy, adolescence, adulthood, and wisdom-maturity. The fourth stage may also be called wisdom-elder.

To be fully mature one must teach others what one has learned and found to be truth. Maturity also requires that those one teaches also teach others to maturity. In this manner an unbroken lineage of spiritual teachers is formed, maintained, and added to.

Wisdom is the full ability to pass on to others the truth that has been gained.

To know another requires sharing one's knowledge, wisdom and experience. Sharing and giving prepares the way for receiving.

Self exists in Mind. Self exists in the three divisions of Mind. The three divisions of Mind are called the Conscious Mind, the Subconscious Mind and the Superconscious Mind.

To know the Self entails knowing Self in all three divisions of Mind. The Subconscious and Superconscious Minds exist at a higher and more refined energy vibratory rate than the Conscious Mind and physical existence. Therefore, the five physical senses do not readily perceive the higher levels of Mind.

To know the Self is to know one's connectedness to all of Mind, all of Creation, and to the Creator. The Creator fashioned all his creation out of LIGHT. To know this creation through connectedness is en-LIGHT-en-ment.

Controlling others requires force. Force is not power. Power is the controlled and directed use of the mind for the purpose of creating higher states of enlightenment for Self and others.

Force, when directed against others, is the misuse of energy for the purpose of restricting others. Why would anyone wish to control others? The reason one person would mistakenly want or try to control other people is because of that person's self-conceived limitations and the refusal to change and grow. Growth in Self is needed in order to advance beyond those limitations.

Mastering or conquering the Self requires power because power is the result of will and imagination. One who is to achieve enlightenment must develop the choice making and the imaging making faculty. It is a truth that you become as you think. Therefore, one must employ the will and imagination to continually create mental images of expansive growth and enlightenment in the Self.

He who knows he has enough is rich because he has achieved desirelessness. This is contentment. Such a one has learned the lesson of physical sensation and found physical life to be of a temporary nature.

There is a strong inner urge to build permanent, lasting, eternal, immortal, peace, love and LIGHT within the Self. Therefore, such a one is rich and builds up treasures in Heaven. This is true and lasting wealth.

The one who listens to, follows, and obeys this inner urge consistently, moves forward in the quickening of the inner Self. Such a one stills the mind and has full awareness of existence as Self, as I AM. Such a one knows and lives the true purpose of life and therefore, achieves prosperous success.

The illusion of physical distance comes to be understood for one lives the union of connectedness. Your rightful place is connectedness. In constant, continual awareness is one's place to endure.

To live, to be present, and fully conscious in the now is eternal life. There is no death in present consciousness. In the eternal now exists all life.

Such a one does not die which is the cessation of consciousness. Instead, the enlightened live in continual, connected consciousness.

The lesson is:

There is always the choice of living only for physical life, sometimes called the lower path, or living for the higher mind and the High Self. The choice is to live for what is temporary or to live for what is lasting, continuous, and eternal.

Which do you choose?

A thinker chooses the greater riches. Eternal life is a continuum of consciousness.

Thirty-four

The Great Tao is all pervading and flows everywhere
to the left and to the right
It gives life force to everything and everyone
and denies no one
The Tao is eternal
and brings all things to completion
without them even knowing it
so we call it small or insignificant
Everything returns to it
yet it does not control them
So we call it The Great

Thus, the Sage in the same way achieves greatness
because he does not claim greatness
He can therefore achieve greatness

34

The replacement for control is the use of the free movement of consciousness. This chapter continues the theme of chapter 33 further explaining the factor or quality of control.

Life force from Superconscious Mind flows constantly to all three divisions of Mind in fulfillment of the divine and Perfect Plan of Creation held in Superconscious Mind.

Life force flows from Superconscious Mind to every person, place and thing in the physical universe. All life and all existence depends upon it. Life force is always supplying its energy and LIGHT at all times. It nourishes everything. Yet creation proceeds according to the Perfect Plan of Creation held in Superconscious Mind and the free choice of each I AM.

All energy, all substance, all objects proceed from Superconscious Mind and to Superconscious Mind they will return. It is the story revealed symbolically in the Bible as the prodigal son in *Luke 15:11-32.* Everything returns to the place from where it came. Yet it is the movement forward in consciousness for one can never go back. The nature of Mind is forward motion.

Life force does not have an individual I AM or ego. Therefore, it cannot be egotistical. Nor can it be selfish, insecure, jealous, or angry. Life force gives of itself to all, at all times, to any receptacle that does not block it or push it away.

Thus, life force is great.

The Sage has achieved greatness because of Self discipline, discipline of the mind, and surrender of the conscious ego. Discipline enables one to give and receive freely. Surrender enables the elimination of mental walls or barriers to the free giving and receiving of knowledge, understanding, and wisdom. The prodigal son left home, made many mistakes including squandering his inheritance on temporary physical gratification. Yet, he gained in wisdom and realized the value of his father's house and home.

It is the duty of each of us to recognize the permanent and lasting value of our Heavenly Father's house that has many mansions. The prodigal son surrendered his ego and swallowed his pride to return to his father. Each of us must also surrender the ego. Because of the surrender of the ego, the Sage is great. The Sage, the thinker has yielded to a higher calling. Such a one achieves greatness by being open to learning and open minded while also giving freely of the wisdom and enlightenment of Self.

The lesson is:

The one who earnestly desires enlightenment
will be open to being taught
and open to receiving learning.
The one who earnestly desires enlightenment
will also give often.

Yield and surrender the conscious ego.

Thirty-five

Hold fast to the Great Image
and the whole world will be attracted to you
be beyond harm
in safety, peace and abundance

Fine food and music
entice the passing travelers to stop
Yet, when the Way is expressed verbally we say
how plain and without flavor it is
We look at it and do not see
We listen to it and do not hear
Yet, when used the Way is inexhaustible

We now advance to the replacement of control which is holding fast to the Image.

To image is to use the imagination. *Genesis 1:1-3, "God created the Heavens and the Earth in the very beginning. And the Earth was without form, and void; and the darkness was upon the face of the deep. And the spirit of God moved upon the face of the water. And God said, 'Let there be LIGHT; and there was LIGHT'."*

Before one can speak words that have meaning, one must first have formed an image in the Mind. Thus, all creations begin with a thought-image. This is universally true whether it is the creation of words, actions, or physical buildings.

The Great Image referred to by Lao Tzu is the image of Self as an en-LIGHT-ened creator. This is for the purpose of fulfilling Self as an offspring of the Creator, endowed with the imaging capability and inner urge to be like the Creator.

All physical experiences are temporary. Therefore, exist and function well in physical life while keeping the consciousness expanded to include the Subconscious and Superconscious Minds. This will place one beyond harm in safety, peace and connectedness.

Fine food and music represent sensory stimuli. Yet the Way of High Knowledge and en-LIGHT-enment is not concerned with engrossment in the senses. The senses, used correctly, are for the purpose of receiving experiences into the brain that may then be reasoned with by the mind. In this way new permanent understandings of creation may be added to the whole Self. This is why physically minded people think the disciplined life is plain or without flavor.

A verse similar to the statement, *"We listen and do not hear"* is found in the Bible, *Revelation 2:29* which says, *"He who has ears, let him hear what the spirit says to the churches."* To listen and not hear is to receive truth into the brain yet refuse to use that truth in the life. To use Universal Truth in the life is to fulfill subconscious mind, the soul, and go beyond the brain.

The energy of Superconscious Mind is inexhaustible because life force is continually being given to both the Subconscious and Conscious Mind. This life force is then continuously returned or recycled back into Mind from physical existence. The planet Earth has energy wheels known as chakras that function to return or recycle this inexhaustible energy from the physical world into the inner levels of Mind so that it may be used again.

Each soul's physical body also has seven chakras that function to return used energy back into Mind. The one who is open to learning and growing in awareness has chakras that are functioning efficiently. Such a one therefore, has great energy.

The lesson is:

Image or imagine the Self as en-LIGHT-ened.
Hold fast to this image. Refine and improve
this image. Live this image until
the Self has become what has been imaged
which is enlightenment.
Breathe life force into Self.

Thirty-six

When you desire to contract a creation
you must temporarily expand it
When you desire to weaken a creation
you must temporarily strengthen it
When you desire to reject a creation
you must temporarily accept it
When you desire to receive a creation
you must temporarily give it
This is called subtle awareness
The submissive and yielding
conquer the stiff and forceful

A fish that ventures out of the watery depths is soon
caught
A country that reveals its weapons is soon conquered

Contract and expand are opposites.

Weaken and strengthen are opposites.

Reject and accept are opposites.

Receive and give are opposites.

Each pair is the two halves of a cycle. As you give so you shall receive. Nature and all of Mind seek to restore balance. Karma is the Law of Balance. When one gives freely there is created an imbalance. Receiving then brings one forward into a greater balance than before one gave.

The physically minded person thinks that in order to get something it has to be taken.

The spiritually minded person realizes and understands that in order to receive something one must first give to a high degree.

In order to master a subject or an aspect of Self one must first give that quality to other people, places, and things.

To expand a creation, to strengthen a creation, to accept a creation, to give a creation are all ways to give, to help, to add to what already exists in one's environment.

In this manner one prepares to receive its other half. In giving, one prepares the Self to be able to receive more than one has previously.

The strong do not conquer the strong. Just as force does not overcome force. Both only destroy. They do not create.

Gautama the Buddha, as quoted in the *Dharmapada* said, *"Hatred can never put an end to hatred; love alone can. This is an unalterable Law"* (1:6).

Jesus the Christ as quoted in the Bible said: *"You have heard that it is said, an eye for an eye and and tooth for a tooth, but I say to you that you should not resist evil; but whoever strikes you on your right cheek, turn to him the other also. But I say to you, love your enemies, bless anyone who curses you, do good to anyone who hates you, and pray for those who carry you away by force and persecute you,"* (Matthew 5:38-39).

Each individual's true nature is love, truth and Light. Just as a fish cannot survive long when taken out of water so our spiritual or Real Self cannot survive when the attention is removed from the depths of Mind for this makes us physically minded.

A State's greatest weapons are not meant to be displayed for these are the tools of force and control. As such, they are only temporary solutions and do not bring lasting happiness nor permanent creation.

The lesson is:

If you want something you must first give it.

In order to accurately perceive and create one must be willing to experience both the aggressive and receptive. Focus on and live the life according to what is lasting and real.

Thirty-seven

The Tao is eternally formless
If rulers and leaders were to live it
everyone would change and transform naturally
If after being transformed should their desires arise
The ruler would still them with formless simplicity
Being stilled by formless simplicity
they would not desire
not desiring they will be at peace in stillness
In stillness one finds the anchor of the universe
within Self

The unformed substance of life force from Superconscious Mind as it moves into the Subconscious or Universal Mind always exists waiting to be acted upon by the thoughts of the individual.

This substance in the Subconscious Mind is a manifestation of the cosmic energy and Divine Plan of Creation held in Superconscious Mind.

The one whose thoughts are clear and productive accomplishes more with less physical action.

When there is harmony and connectedness to all creation in the thoughts, then all grow and mature in harmony with the divine plan of Creation. Then there is joy and fulfillment in creating with love of connectedness.

Then all activity, all actions are performed with the greatest results for all is in harmony with the Divine Plan.

To go against this Divine Plan is to produce pain. To act and think in harmony with the Divine Plan produces the blissful love of connectedness that leads to oneness of ideal.

All the universe is energy. What is referred to and thought of as form, is only energy slowed down or in a condensed state perceivable to the five senses.

Desire springs from the urge to control energy. Desires are the misguided attempts to gain power by controlling what is wrongly perceived as separate from the Self. Desires relate to the temporariness and impermanence of form.

Needs express as an urge to understand the use of energy in order to gain an understanding of permanence, externality, and immortality.

When the urge to control those things that are temporary is overcome and transcended, the Self achieves universal peace and bliss. Such a one exists in the joy of fulfillment.

In this way all may exist in harmony and peace.

In this way the Self can achieve fulfillment.

To allow the free movement of consciousness while directing it with life force gives Self and others the opportunity to let go the restrictions and limitations to form which is to transform.

When one realizes the ability to create the life as one wills and images it then the mind is free to be still and quiet.

When the environment is not peaceful it is difficult to stop the thoughts of Self from running and rushing through the mind. When one feels fulfilled it is much easier to have a still mind.

From a still mind comes peace of mind.

From a still, quiet, and peaceful mind one is able to align the conscious and subconscious minds symbolized by Earth and attune both to Superconscious Mind as symbolized by Heaven.

The lesson is:

**Receive the cosmic energy
life force into the Self. Breath it in.
Seek to understand the movement of thought,
energy, and consciousness instead of getting bogged
down in physical experiences and physical objects.**

**Be at peace and align
one's conscious and subconscious minds and
attune them to Superconscious Mind.**

Thirty-eight

The Superior power does not display this power
For this reason such a one has power
The inferior power will not forget about power
For this reason such a one is without power
The highest power is to act without a sense of Self
the highest kindness is to give without condition
the highest justice is to perceive without favoritism
but when the physical rules of conduct are not followed
people are seized by the arm and rules forced upon them

Therefore, when the Way (Tao) is lost
rules of virtue appear
when virtue is lost rules of kindness appear
when kindness is lost rules of justice appear
when justice is lost rules of conduct appear
Rules of conduct mark the waning
of belief and trustworthiness
and the beginning of confusion of the heart
Relying on rules for guidance
is only the flowery covering of the Way
and the beginning of delusion

Therefore, The Great Spiritual Master resides in the Real
and does not dwell on the surface
and resides in the fullness of Reality
and does not dwell in the flowery, outer covering
Therefore, receive what is within and reject what is
without

The attention of the individual, when undisciplined, can move farther away from the soul and more and more into sensory engrossment. This passage is concerned with outlining the manner in which this occurs.

The Higher Consciousness seems to descend from the Way to virtue, to kindness, to justice, to ritual, to rules, until finally the people rebel against the rules and are then controlled by force.

Rules never give belief or Self trust nor do they open the heart to love or understanding.

Rules give form and structure only. It is for the thinker to use the form and structure productively. Rules are of the surface or physical world. They promote physical thinking.

The fullness of reality is the permanent understanding of Self and creation gained from each experience and added to one's soul which is one's subconscious mind.

A productive, responsible thinker always seeks to add to whatever good is in the environment. He is not satisfied with yesterday's accomplishments. Rather such a one listens to the inner urge for enlightenment and pursues it.

Pretending to be productive, pretending to live according to Universal Law will not enhance one's soul growth. Only complete giving of the Self and complete receiving into the Self will cause this.

Enlightenment comes not from activity. Rather enlightenment comes from the still mind and the intention to learn and grow, in and through, the action and effort.

You can dig ditches for a thousand years and still not be enlightened. Or you can be an enlightened ditch digger.

The attention must always be on adding to one's permanent storehouse of knowledge.

The truly kind person seeks to aid others knowing full well that "as you give so you shall receive." Therefore, such a one is able to give completely of the Self.

A just person tries to promote justice which implies the attention is always on the crime when instead the attention needs to be on soul growth and spiritual development.

The physical thinking person attempts to use force to make others do things without purpose. Therefore, such a person is constantly trying to misuse control rather than understanding power.

The Tao is the Light of Creation. It is the perfect seed idea of Creation manifesting through the levels of Mind through the agency of Life Force.

Kindness is indicated by the phrase *"Love your neighbor as yourself."* This is related to the Golden Rule of the Bible, as given by Jesus the Christ and other great spiritual masters, *"Do unto others as you would have them do unto you."* Justice is a physical attempt to try to make people get along with each other without the understanding of Universal Law.

Force is the blind attempt of some outside, or unknown power to control the Self. It is often devoid of the practical use of will power and imagination.

The future has yet to arrive. There is only the eternal now. Power which derives from the understanding of Creation is in the now.

What is real is the now. What is real is thought and effect is its manifest likeness.

Learn how to think. The purpose of rules is to aid a person to learn the thinking process and live in the now. Be in the present and create rather than being entrapped in the sensory stimulus and momentary gratification.

The lesson is:

Gain the learning in every experience without becoming sensory engrossed in the experience. Improve the thinking ability every day.

131

Thirty-nine

Of things that attained oneness in ancient times of long ago
Heaven achieved oneness and thereby became clear
Earth achieved oneness and thereby becoming stabilized
Minds achieved oneness and thereby became divine
Streams achieved oneness and thereby became full
Leaders and Kings achieved oneness
      and ruled the whole land correctly

Therefore, given this knowledge it implies that
the clarity of Heaven-the sky,
      prevents it from splitting open
the stability of Earth prevents it from shaking
the divinity of the mind prevents it from ceasing to be
the fullness of the stream prevents it from drying up
the productivity of leaders and Kings prevents their
      downfall

Thus, value has as its root humbleness
the low is the foundation for the high
for this reason nobles and Kings refer to themselves
orphaned, widowed and destitute
but is this the basis of true humility?

Therefore, they act as if their large numbers of carriages
are the same as having no carriages
For this reason do not wish to sparkle and glitter like jade
Instead remain strong and lasting like a rock

The first creation of the Creator was LIGHT. From LIGHT was created individualized units of LIGHT called I AM or plural I AMs. Each I AM was endowed by their Creator with the choice making ability and individuality.

All creation is connected. It is not separate. The illusion of separateness, of distance, and therefore time is called Maya.

Each individual is one whole being but because of illusion or Maya we tend to see ourselves as separate, unconnected and isolated. Yet the truth is, we are all connected and what we do to others we do to ourselves.

Heaven or sky symbolizes Superconscious Mind. Earth symbolizes the Conscious and Subconscious Minds. The Mind or spirit is I AM manifesting or existing in all levels of Mind.

The Stream symbolizes the Conscious Mind and life experiences being used productively by the thinker to produce permanent soul understandings of Creation.

All aspects of Self can be used fully by the thinker.

The goal of Self is wholeness, which is to understand and use the whole mind and to unite all aspects of Self into an enlightened being. This is the greatest virtue.

Clear perception is created by the still mind. The still mind is the key to knowing Superconscious Mind.

Earth, being Subconscious Mind, and the physical environment gives us the way and place to develop as creators.

Mind, which is the vehicle I AM uses in order to experience and learn, is continually motivating Self to grow and mature as a creator.

The most highly developed aspects of Self continually urge the conscious mind forward to learn and grow. Humbleness is the greatest honesty. Self honesty is the foundation of all soul growth and spiritual development for truth and love rule the universe and serve under the eternal LIGHT of the Creator. Honesty leads to truth and truth leads to Universal Truth.

Physical existence is the part of mind extended farthest from the Creator's LIGHT. The rate of vibration of energy has been slowed or lengthened. Thus the unenlightened consider themselves widowed, destitute, and orphaned.

Appearances can be deceiving. The senses will fool you. The conscious mind will lie to you.

Therefore, do not pretend to be something other than what you are as given in the example of the nobles who pretended that their large number of carriages and possessions were the same as having no possessions.

Those things that glitter and sparkle represent the countless numbers of sensory experiences and objects that can stimulate physical desires. Accumulating physical desires by itself is a dead end. Soul growth is only produced when soul learning is received in the experience. This soul learning is called understanding or the plural understandings.

Rather than getting engrossed in physical desires instead remain committed to the ideal of enlightenment. Use will power as symbolized by the rock to produce this enlightenment.

The lesson is:

Surrender the conscious ego by practicing humbleness.

Use the will to produce a still mind.
Be committed to unifying all of Mind
and all of one's consciousness into a unified whole
that is called en-LIGHT-en-ment.

Forty

The movement of the Tao is to return
The Way of the Tao is to yield

The things of the world come from being
in physical existence
Being in physical existence comes from not being
in physical existence

When the energy that has been sent forth returns there is a complete cycle.

All life force from Superconscious Mind is used by souls in the Subconscious and Conscious Minds. Then it returns to Superconscious Mind to be recycled and sent forth again.

It is the Perfect Plan of Creation for there to be infinite energy. In order to unite the many thousands of aspects of Self into a unified whole in alignment with I AM, infinite energy is required. The more one creates, the more one understands Creation. The more one understands Creation, the more energy is available.

To receive the energy of the Creator, which is infinite, one must surrender the conscious ego, for the conscious ego – which perceives through the five senses and brain – views Self as separate from the world. The illusion of separation never gives power.

Thus, yielding is the way to know Creation, all of Mind and the Mind of the Creator.

A still mind receives and therefore yields.

A humble Self can receive and therefore yields, learns, and grows.

Each has power because both are connected.

The thousands of aspects of Self derive form from the soul being born into physical existence with its accompanying sensory engrossment which produces false and separate thinking.

The illusionary physical life of separation, isolation, distance, and time is an extension of the true existence of complete connectedness.

The infinite power of infinite connectedness of being is sometimes referred to as not being or not being in form, or non-existence.

The statement *"the movement of the Tao is to return"* indicates the life force energy is recycled. The life force that comes from LIGHT is beyond form. All life, form, and existence in Mind and physical existence owes itself to this. The great enlightened being Pythagoras who taught the truths upon which Western science and much of Western civilization is based, said in The Golden Verses of Pythagoras, *"Never start on your task until you have implored the blessing of the Gods. If this you hold fast, soon you will recognize of Gods and mortal men the true nature of existence, how everything passes and returns. Then you will see what is true, how Nature in all is most equal."*

The LIGHT of the Creator becomes life force in Superconscious Mind and then moves into Subconscious Mind where it begins to take on form. Then it moves to the physical world where we experience this LIGHT as physical objects and forms. Then the energy and mind substance deteriorate in the physical world and return or recycle into Subconscious Mind to be used again and again.

The lesson is:

Use experiences to the fullest by using every opportunity to add to one's soul growth and spiritual development. When the lesson is learned the life force and substance can be returned and recycled to be used again in a different form.

Forty-One

When the superior thinker hears the Way
he practices it with commitment
When the average thinker hears of the Way
he thinks of it now and then
When the inferior thinker hears the Way
he laughs at it loudly
If he did not laugh it would not be the Way

From this comes an old saying:
The bright way seems dark
the forward way seems backward
the smoothest way seems rough
the highest virtue seems low
the purest white seems black
the highest power seems empty
Abundant power seems inadequate
Truth and reality seem to change
the perfect square has no corners
the perfect vessel is never filled
the perfect note makes little sound
the perfect image has no shape

The Tao is hidden and has no form
only the Tao is good at beginning
and good at completing.

The Superior thinker disciplines the mind through concentration and meditation exercises. The superior thinker lives a life of disciplined commitment to knowing the whole Self and creation. Therefore, a disciplined thinker, the superior thinker always has the mind open in order to receive any possibility of greater truth.

The average thinker hears the truth with the sense of hearing through the ears, receives the truth through the sense of sight in the form of the written word, and thinks about it. Yet, such a one does not initiate the choice making ability to cause any forward movement in consciousness. The average thinker usually lacks a willingness to quicken soul growth and spiritual development.

The inferior thinker is caught up and engrossed with sensory experiences of the temporal life and is therefore a firm believer in the separateness of life. To such a one the true nature of reality which is universal connectedness seems strange and absurd.

In the Bhagavad Gita the superior thinker is said to be functioning from Sattvas Guna.

The average thinker is said to be Rajas Guna.

The inferior thinker given in the Tao Te Ching is the same as Tamas Guna given in the Bhagavad Gita, Chapter 14.

The three Gunas or Principles of Nature are called the three qualities. They are:

Sattvas or truth = the superior thinker
Rajas or passion = the average thinker
Tamas or indifference = the inferior thinker

Instead of dividing the types of thinker into three categories, Jesus who became Christed divides the thinker into four categories given in the parable of the seed. He even explains the types of thinking and reasoning or lack of reasoning involved.

"And when many people had gathered and were coming to him from all the cities, he spoke in parables. A sower went out to sow his seed. And when he had sown, some seed fell on the roadside; and it was trodden underfoot, and the birds ate it. Other seed fell upon the rock and sprang up quickly, and because it had no moisture, it dried up. And other seed fell among thistles and the thistles sprang up with it and choked it. And other seed fell in good and fertile ground; and sprang up and bore fruit a hundredfold. And when he said this, he cried out, He who has ears to hear, let him hear.

"And his disciples asked him, What is this parable?

"He said to them, To you it is granted to know the mystery of the kingdom of God; but to the rest, it has to be said in figures; for while they see, they do not perceive; and while they hear, they do not understand.

"This is the parable: The seed is the word of God.

"Those on the roadside are those who hear the words, and the enemy comes and takes away the word from their hearts, so that they may not believe and be saved. Those on the rock are those who when they have heard, receive the word with joy; and yet they have no root, but their belief is for a while, and in time of trial they stumble. That which fell among the thistles are those who heard the word, and then choke themselves with worries and riches and worldly covetousness, and bear no fruit. But that in good, soil, these are those who hear the word with a pure and good heart, and keep it, and bear fruit with patience.

"No man lights a lamp and covers it with a vessel, or puts it under the bed; but he puts is on the lampstand that whoever enters sees its light. For there is nothing covered which will not be uncovered; and nothing hidden which will not be known and come to light. Take heed how you hear; for he who has, to him shall be given; and from him who has not, even that which he thinks he has shall be taken away," (Luke 8:4-17).

The bright way seems dark in this chapter because the bright way involves letting go of false values and false securities. It involves reaching for something beyond the five senses, something unseen.

The one who is engrossed in the senses thinks that the forward way is greater accumulation of physical objects. The truth is all of these are temporary. Therefore, the attention and effort needs to be upon building permanent understandings of Self, Mind, and all creation.

The disciplined life which is the smoothest way at first seems rough. Once one learns and masters Self discipline, life becomes much easier and simpler.

The highest virtue such as practicing the statement *"as you give so shall you reap"* seems low because an entrapped, physical thinking person is under the illusion that Self is separate from all creation. By this type of thinking a person wrongly thinks to lose if something such as money is given to another. For them the money is separate from the person who gave. The Real Truth is, because of Universal Connectedness, it is only by giving that one may receive.

The highest learning is the study of Mind and Self for Mind is the tool or vehicle for knowing the Self. The highest division of Mind is Superconscious Mind. The highest and Real Self is I AM. The Tao is the Perfect Plan of Creation manifesting from Superconscious Mind through Subconscious Mind to Conscious Mind, the physical world. The Plan is for each I AM to mature into an enlightened being, a creator.

The Superior Thinker, the one with a strong inner urge to know the Self, upon hearing truth, applies it. By applying and living truth such a one comes to know Universal Truth. The spiritual thinker who is the Superior Thinker has a strong inner urge to know Self. This knowledge and understanding of the whole Self is unceasing as the Superior Thinker pursues soul growth and spiritual development.

The average or human thinker, reads or hears words of Universal Laws, Universal Truths, and Universal Principles yet only thinks about these truths now and then. This kind of person may even continue to read books about Metaphysics, Mind, and Universal Truth.

The inferior thinker, the one engrossed in the five senses and physical thinking, is a slave to the senses and therefore does not recognize the value of anything the eyes can not see. The Bible says, *"Let them who have eyes see. Let those who have ears hear"* *(Revelation 3:13).*

All physical life is the play of Maya, which is illusion. It is not that physical life is an illusion. Physical life is very real. It is the average or inferior thinker's perception of physical life that is incorrect or illusory for the five senses delude the sensory engrossed being into thinking all is temporary and the Self is separate. These conceptions are false.

The play of life is joyous when one can perceive the truth of things.

The bright path seems dim to the inferior thinker because it runs contrary to accepted norms. What is normal to human man is incredibly limiting and therefore abnormal to spiritual man.

What is obviously truth to a spiritual, intuitive thinker seems non-existent for one engrossed in the physical experiences.

During the first stages of commitment to the full spiritual life it may seem to the student that he is losing something. That previous investment in physical life is wasted. This is illusion. What is actually occurring is the student is trading in what is temporary for something lasting, permanent and eternal.

The *Book of Matthew* in the Bible says, *"Seek ye first the kingdom of Heaven and all these things will be added to you"* *(Matthew 6:33).* The Bible does not say seek ye first the kingdom of Heaven and a;l else will immediately be added unto you. Yet the one who perseveres will fulfill one's mission in life and find their true inner desires are realized. At first the way may seem more difficult because mental discipline is required. Yet the sincere, disciplined student does find and create greater fulfillment. Virtues which are Universal Truths become, through practice, real in the life and in the Self.

The perfect square that has no corner is a circle which symbolizes continual forward motion in consciousness which is the goal of all true mental thinkers.

The perfect vessel is never filled for a Superior Thinker

keeps continually giving and therefore receiving. Since such a one constantly gives and thus never fills up. Yet the cup of Self for such a one keeps getting larger and larger until all the riches of the Universe flow into and through such a one.

The greatest spirituality does not always appear early in life but takes time to mature. The perfect note is OM and it sounds eternally. OM sounds eternally in the silence. Those who have mastered the still mind can hear and perceive the OM. Those who go deep in meditation can hear the OM.

The perfect image has no shape because that image is beyond the Subconscious and Conscious Minds and is therefore beyond form. The perfect image is of Superconscious Mind and is therefore, pure consciousness and life force energy. The life force from Superconscious Mind makes life possible in the physical world. It is the source of all energy and power.

The Tao is hidden in Superconscious Mind. The Tao is the Alpha and Omega, the beginning and the end as given in the *Bible. Revelation 1:8, "I AM the Alpha and Omega, the beginning and the ending says the Lord God, who is and who was and who is to come, the Almighty."* The Aramaic words for Alpha and Omega are Aleph and Tau. Aramaic was the original language of the Bible.

The lesson is:

Be open minded and receive the truth. Be committed to internalizing Universal Truth. Constantly strive to know the greater hidden truth.

143

Forty-two

The Tao gives birth to the One
One gives birth to the Two
Two gives birth to the Three
The Three gives birth to ten thousand things
The Ten thousand things are sustained by Yin
and are embraced by Yang
the eternal breath between them creates harmony
and the interaction of these two factors fills the
universe

What all under Heaven hate most
is to be orphaned, widowed, or destitute
Yet this is how Kings and nobles describe themselves
Thus, sometimes beings lose something
but sometimes gain something else

Thus, the ancient lesson that others teach
I receive and teach also, which is
the violent and forceful do not die a natural death
I use this as the foundation of my teachings

All creation proceeds from the Creator's light of awareness.
There is one LIGHT. From this one LIGHT came individualized units of LIGHT called I AM. I AM is also one in that it is
individual.

From LIGHT proceeded the Perfect Plan of Creation held
in Superconscious Mind. The tools for fulfilling this plan are the
Aggressive and Receptive Principles of Creation held in
Superconscious Mind.

These two principles of creation which are the yin and
yang of the Tao Te Ching, together create or give birth to a third.
This third is the child. It is the progeny of the Aggressive and
Receptive Principles of Creation.

This three that is created out of the two then creates with
other threes to create the thousands of aspects of the Self and the
many faceted creative process of mind.

When the male and female, the aggressive and receptive,
can create a third form then creation can proceed. Creation is
continual and eternal.

The ten thousand things are sustained by yin because yin
is the receptive principle of Creation. The quality of the receptive principle is expectant non-action. Yin is nurturing. Yin is
also associated with female, dark, absorbing, valleys, and streams.

Yang embraces the ten thousand things because yang is
the aggressive principle of creation. The quality of the aggressive
quality is to initiate motion-activity.

The Aggressive and Receptive Principles of Creation combine to create harmony. Through harmony they create a child, a
third, an expanding creation.

The person who gets caught up in physical possessions,
becoming ensnared by the distractions of limitations and temporariness, separates Self mentally from all creation. The one who
separates and isolates loses power. The egoic one separates. The

one who connects gains power. Power is in connectedness. Love creates connectedness. Too much Yin creates a busy mind. A busy conscious mind is unable to listen and know the inner Self. *"Then Jesus said to him, 'Return the sword to its place; for all who take swords will die by swords',"* (Matthew 26:52).

Forsake physical control for the spiritual power of connectedness. He who divides loses power. He who brings together through harmony gains the power of Creation which derives from the One which is connectedness.

Thought is cause. The universe operates in cycles. *"As you sow, so shall you reap."* He who gives receives. To him who has more will be given.

What goes around, comes around. You become as you think. What you do to others you do to yourself. Do unto others as you would have them do unto you.

Most people hate being alone, without friends or without the means to accomplish their goals and desires. Connectedness is the essence of power, harmony, Love, truth, LIGHT and receptivity. This is the essence of Lao Tzu's teaching.

The lesson is:

*Always seek a balance and harmony
between the aggressive and receptive within the Self.
Continuously create with the aggressive quality
and receive with the receptive quality.*

Forty-three

The softest, most yielding thing in the world
will overcome the hardest, and most rigid
The most empty thing in the world
will overcome the most full
Therefore,
I know there is benefit in expectant non-action
stillness is greater than action
silence is greater than words
Few in the world learn the lessons of
stillness and silence
and gain the abundance and knowledge
of this world

The softest and most yielding thing is flexible, malleable, change-able. The hardest thing is rigid and difficult to change.

Water is soft. Water will mold to any form of vessel it is poured into. Yet, water can cut mighty gorges through mountains and fields.

Throw a rock into a pond filled with water. At first there is a hole where the rock enters the water. Then the water rushes in to fill the space. At first there are waves then all returns to tranquility.

A rock placed in a stream of moving water will be worn smooth.

This is why the softest thing overcomes the hardest thing.

Air can enter a room filled with people or furniture. Fish enter a pond that is filled with water. Hence the more refined the vibration of anything the more its goodness and LIGHT are able to permeate the world.

This is the value of receptivity. One who is receptive can harmonize with the environment including the people in the environment. One who is receptive fills the void of spaces not being used or occupied thereby creating a more enriching and fulfilling experience for all.

Work without emotional attachment to the activity or the physical goal. Rather create an ideal of spiritual transformation in all you do. Cause accelerated soul growth and spiritual development at all times.

The ability to consciously accelerate soul growth and quicken the enlightenment of the Self is understood by very few. This is why everyone in the physical world needs a spiritual teacher. Such a one aids the student to avoid the pitfalls and dead ends of physical learning focusing instead on permanent understandings being added to the storehouse of Subconscious Mind, the immortal soul.

First there were few teachers of the Mind. Now there are becoming more.

One who disciplines the mind through concentration and meditation understands the value in stilling the mind. In the still mind one can be receptive. Thereby the knowledge and awareness is available in each experience.

Silence enables one to perceive with the mind. The one who is constantly thinking many thoughts will find the thinking is physicalized and localized in the brain. Busy undisciplined thoughts are mostly of the brain and memories stored in the brain.

A person who silences the thoughts can then exist in the stillness of the mind. Having mastered the attention, one can choose the thoughts to be imaged. Then the thinker is capable of using the mind to know consciousness and the Self.

In regards to the power of stillness and silence, the mighty Zarathustra, the Persian Christ had much to say. *"Then did I realize thee as the Most Bountiful One, O Mazda Ahura, when the Good Mind encircled me completely. He declared to me that silent meditation is the best for attaining spiritual enlightenment," (Yasna 43.15)*

In order to gain enlightenment, one must learn to discipline the mind so that it will become a worthy servant, tool, or vehicle for Self awareness. It is through the still mind that the understanding of the true reality of universal connectedness is known. The busy mind remains engrossed in the senses and sensory experiences. The five senses give the false impression or illusion of separateness and isolation. The still mind enables one to experience the true reality of connectedness and oneness.

The lesson is:

The receptive, still mind that then produces a creative imaged thought is the great power of the universe. A still mind learns how to learn the great lessons of life and how to know the Real Self.

Forty-four

Fame or health
which is most important
Health or riches
which is more valuable
Gain or loss
which is more harmful
The more excessive the attachment to desires
the greater the suffering
The larger the treasure
the greater the loss

Therefore, know when you have enough
and experience no humiliation
Know disciplined restraint
and experience no trouble
In this way one can live a very long time

44

Health is more important than fame. Fame is fleeting and temporary. When one has health one can pursue soul growth and the quickening of enlightenment. The Buddha is quoted in the Dhammapada 15:204 as saying, *"Health is the best gift, contentment the best wealth, trust is the best kinsman, nirvana is the greatest joy."*

Fame, at best, lasts a lifetime. A person can be famous one lifetime and the next lifetime, when not famous, study unwittingly about the past life when fame was achieved.

Physical riches are also temporary. They last, at best, a lifetime. Health can be used in conjunction with the mind to produce great Self awareness and understanding. When health is lost it is difficult to enjoy wealth or pursue soul growth and Self awareness.

Either gain or loss may be painful. It depends upon what one does with experience. If one uses the gain to help others it can be beneficial. If one is selfish with gain then the result is suffering. Loss may seem harmful. Yet often it stimulates us to go deeper into ourselves to tap that reservoir of talent and wisdom within. At times such as these we may go beyond previously accepted limitations.

Gautama the Buddha said, *"Those who are selfish suffer in this life and the next. They suffer seeing the results of the evil they have done, and more suffering awaits them in the next life. But those who are selfless rejoice in this life and the next. They rejoice seeing the good that they have done and more joy awaits them in the next life,"* (*Dharmapada 1:17-18*).

The Bible says, *"The love of money is the root of all evil,"* (*Timothy 6:10*). It does not say money is the root of all evil. Excessive love or attachment to money is greed. Hoarding treasures is a form of selfishness. Treasure or value or valuables are meant to be used. The greatest use is sharing.

To allow physical wealth or objects to hold or control the attention is to miss out on the opportunity for quickening soul growth. The larger the physical treasure the more temptation to be distracted and engrossed in the physical senses and physical experiences.

Therefore, see to your needs and see to other's needs. Your desires are limitless. Your needs are few. A disciplined mind has the power and ability to practice restraint. A disciplined mind does not have to go to extremes and thereby avoids trouble.

When one avoids extremes one is free to receive the mind learning in every situation. As one continues to learn and grow in consciousness there is purpose and meaning to life. As long as one has purpose for living so does one promote longevity in Self.

The lesson is:

The physical body is the vehicle the soul uses to build permanent understandings of Self and creation. Use it wisely.

Forty-five

Great perfection seems imperfect
yet the world it creates is never exhausted
The Great Fullness seems empty
yet the world it creates is never used up

Great truth seems wrong
Great intelligence seems stupid
Great wealth of eloquence
     seems like poor communication

Motion overcomes cold
Stillness overcomes heat
Stillness and peace
enable one to bring order to the world

45

The physical sensations that seem to offer fulfillment prove to be temporary and illusory. Physical experiences seem empty to a soul that hungers and thirsts for the real inner meaning of life. Even though the soul entrapped in a physical body yearns for more than physical experience, it seems as if the physical world goes on and on with incredible resources.

Attitudes that create worldly success do not necessarily produce mental success or success of the mind. This is why great truth seems wrong and great intelligence seems stupid.

Great wealth seems poor because it is temporary. Wealth comes and goes or else the physical body comes and goes. Most people live less than 70 or 80 years and then die meaning that the soul's attention is withdrawn from the physical body. So to have something that is temporary as one's main motivator in life seems ridiculous. The only reasonable motivation is to pursue, gain, learn, know, and build within the Self that which is permanent and lasting. Great eloquence seems poor in communication when the listener is physically minded and refuses to receive and hear the Higher Truths presented by the Sage.

Perfection does not exist in the physical world because perfection is not of this world. Perfection is of Superconscious Mind which holds the balance of the Aggressive and Receptive Principles of Creation and the Perfect Plan of Creation. The yin and yang, the aggressive and receptive principles of creation, is the mechanism by which the Perfect Plan of Creation is fulfilled.

Great accomplishments in the physical world are imperfect because they are temporary. Everything of the physical universe is constantly deteriorating. It is called entropy or rate of rot.

The Superconscious Mind, I AM, LIGHT, LOVE, permanent soul understandings of creation and Universal Truths are all eternal. Perfection is intimately connected to eternal truths, eternal or Universal Laws, eternal or Universal Principles, and the LIGHT of awareness which is of the Creator.

Yet temporary physical forms and structures have their usefulness. They serve as a vehicle or opportunity for each person to learn and grow in order to mature as an enlightened being, a creator.

All the sensory experiences only give temporary satisfaction. Yet they offer no fulfillment. One who fills the belly with food finds that a few hours later hunger is once again experienced. In contrast, soul growth and spiritual development are ever-fulfilling and ever-renewing.

Accomplishing physical goals does not always beget spiritual ideals. However, there is no end to learning Metaphysical truths and incorporating these truths into the enlightenment of the Self.

Reading books and memorizing information is food for the brain or brain food. It leads to intellectualism.

To apply information from books in one's life leads to awareness. To reason with the expansive experience leads to knowledge.

To receive the teachings of the Universal Laws from a teacher enables one to learn, to reason.

To teach what one has learned to others leads to wisdom.

To discipline the Self and the Mind with concentration, meditation, visualization, dream interpretation and giving as taught by a teacher, leads one to enlightenment.

Saying great words is good. Applying them in the life is better. Teaching others to do so is excellent.

Motion generates friction against inertia which produces heat thereby overcoming cold.

The quiet, still mind reduces the friction of the mind in motion and thereby reduces and overcomes heat.

The still mind causes alignment of the Conscious and Subconscious Minds and an attunement to Superconscious Mind. A still mind is a powerful mind. A busy mind is a weak mind. This alignment brings order for it aligns and connects all in fulfilling the Perfect Plan of Creation in Superconscious Mind. This is the peace and tranquility of fulfilling that Plan and thereby being full of LIGHT called en-LIGHT-en-ment.

The lesson is:

The one who stills the mind
brings order to the world.

Forty-six

When the Tao prevails in the World
swift horses are used to haul manure to the fields
When the Tao does not prevail in the world
war horses are bred on sacred ground

No sin is greater than attachment to desire
No disaster is greater than discontent
No curse brings more sorrow
      than the desire for selfish gain

Therefore,
The understanding that derives
from knowing contentment is eternal fulfillment.

When the perfect Plan of Creation is lived, will power – as symbolized by horses – is used productively. Will power is used to haul manure to the gardens and fields where it is an excellent fertilizer. This fertilizer helps plants to produce food for many. This is creation in motion.

When the Perfect Plan of Creation is ignored and avoided will, stubbornness, and force are misused to destroy instead of to create. War destroys.

The Perfect Plan of Creation is an ever moving forward motion to add to, connect and build.

Desire causes one to be attached to things of the physical world. Attachment creates a stoppage of forward motion. One becomes bound and chained to the object desired.

To misuse sacred ground is to forget or refuse to acknowledge the Universal Laws and Truths. It is the refusal to make the effort to know the Self as more than a physical body. When the individual is following the Tao, which is the Way to enlightenment then the will is used correctly to nurture all productive thoughts as well as to grow greater Self awareness. When the person becomes physical minded then the will is misused and one forgets what is whole and Holy. The Real Inner Self, the whole Mind and the soul are Holy.

The Bhagavad Gita also has a similar statement to make about attachment to desire. *"And those confounded and confused in their minds by reason of their delusions, excesses, and vain living – they become entangled in the nets of their own desires and attachments. And the weight of their objects and attachments, holding them fast, drags them down into the quicksands of Hell, which is the repeated rebirth into the lower and lower planes of the mire and slime of materiality and sensuality," (Chapter 16).*

Gautama the Buddha says, *"Attachment to desire is the cause of all suffering."*

Experiences are to be used for learning and growth in the present time period, in the eternal now. As one forms attachments the person becomes more and more enmeshed in the past. In addition the attachments cause the thinking to become more and more physical and less and less mental or spiritual. The physical world is temporary and limited in its scope. Therefore, attachments to objects of desire or memories of objects of desire can never fulfill the inner Self. Instead these attachments cause time to be wasted when it could be put to better use building new permanent learning of Self and creation.

The energy of experience is to be used and transformed into learning. It is not meant to be held onto for the nature of our physical world is change. Only the Real Self and the Higher Mind is permanent and lasting.

Discontent is the refusal to use the present moment for permanent learning and soul growth. When one is discontented, there is a lack of fulfillment. This lack of fulfillment comes from a refusal to use the opportunities at hand to change, grow, and gain new awareness. It comes from the refusal to change and keep learning. It comes from living in one's memory and wanting things to stay the same. Whereas, the nature of physical existence is change.

Directed change is good.

Selfishness feeds the conscious ego. The conscious ego is your devil. The same ego or devil referred to in *Matthew*, Chapter 4. Service to others expands one's consciousness. Thinking only of oneself limits one's consciousness. Selfishness breeds limitations and restrictions.

Restrictions on giving create restrictions in receiving.

Love of others creates value and worth in the Self.

Joy, happiness, and fulfillment are only found in the expansion of consciousness required to help and aid others.

Look to the needs of oneself more so than the desires. One needs food, shelter and clothing for the physical body. One needs spiritual nourishment for the soul or inner Self. Live life according to Universal Law and Universal Truth, in that order, and all will be well.

The thinker devotes more and more time to knowing Self and aiding others to do the same. Living according to one's needs frees the mind to pursue the spiritual urging within Self that leads to en-LIGHT-enment.

The lesson is:

Look to the needs of Self more than desires.
In everything thought and done include others
and their betterment, their benefit.
This aids in the expansion of consciousness.

Forty-seven

Without going outdoors
one may know all under Heaven
Without looking out windows
one may know the Way of Heaven
The farther one goes
the less one knows

Therefore,
The Sage knows without moving
perceives without looking
achieves without action

47

Heaven symbolizes Superconscious Mind. To know everything under Superconscious Mind one must discipline one's own mind, quiet the thoughts, and expand the consciousness. What exists under Heaven or Superconscious Mind? The answer is the Subconscious and Conscious Divisions of Mind. The Conscious Division of Mind is our physical world and universe.

Knowing Self, all of creation, and all of Mind is not a function of physically traveling from one place to another. It is a function of a disciplined mind. It is not a function of sight or any of the five senses. Enlightenment is created by mastering one's mind and from that all of the three Universes which are also known as the three divisions of Mind. As the mind of Self is mastered it must be employed to know Self in order for a quickening of Self realization.

To travel the world looking for sensory experiences will never bring enlightenment. In many cases it will just build a stronger brain pathway or habit of sensory engrossment.

Therefore, the Sage, the disciplined thinker stills the mind and body, goes within and expands the consciousness. Such a one knows the Self and Mind from direct mental experience and goes beyond the limitations of the five senses.

Such a one perceives with the mind. This perception goes beyond physical eyesight. Such a one goes beyond entrapment in the physical body and more and more is able to achieve with the use of the mind.

The way of Heaven is the plan of Creation held in Superconscious Mind that is striving to manifest through all levels and divisions of Mind.

The reason there is truth to the statement *"the farther one goes the less one knows,"* is because as one grows in consciousness one becomes more aware of divisions of Mind and aspects of the Self that one can learn about, use, and come to know.

Movement is a function of the physical body. Looking is a function of one's physical eyesight. Action is a function of the physical body. The Sage, the enlightened one comes to more and more move the mind as the consciousness is expanded. Such a one perceives with the mind, and achieves power from the initiation of thought which is mental action.

The lesson is:

*A disciplined, still mind leads
to perception, awareness, success and
the full use of all of Mind.*

Forty-eight

The pursuit of learning consists
of adding to every day
The pursuit of the Tao consists of releasing every day
Release and release again
until they perceive nothing to do
so expectant non-action is achieved
nothing is done yet, nothing is left undone

The one who rules the world does not have
a busy mind
the one who has a busy mind is not fit to rule
the world

A true reasoner attempts to add to or build upon whatever exists in the life and in the environment. A reasoner adds to the Self's awareness, reasoning, consciousness, understanding, perception, intuition, and discipline everyday. This is the pursuit of learning. A reasoner causes the life and the environment to be better today than it was yesterday.

The pursuit of the Tao consists of releasing every day. To release is to let go. How can a person release what one is emotionally attached to? The answer is to transform the energy to a higher truth. All limitations in consciousness must be transformed into a more expanded consciousness. Emotional attachments must be released. Hatreds, angers, fears, doubts, guilts, resentments, jealousies and avoidance must be released. When all of these limitations are released by the act of transforming the mind and consciousness by learning the universal lessons of life then all work is complete. Total receptivity is achieved. Nothing is left undone in the physical life because there are no karmic ties to bind the soul to the physical body and the cycle of reincarnation.

Most so-called learning is in fact information stored in the brain. It is brain food or food for thought. Day by day, year by year, the non-enlightened individual adds more stored memories of physical, sensory experiences to the brain.

The one who is striving for quickened soul growth and spiritual development is more concerned with using the mind, the whole mind than just the physical organ called the brain.

Learning to use the mind is a process of learning to quiet the mind. When the sincere student develops the still mind then the whole mind becomes known. The whole Mind includes Conscious, Subconscious and Superconscious Minds.

In pursuit of fulfilling the Perfect Plan of Creation held in Superconscious Mind distractions and limitations of physical life are released. The Mind expands beyond physical desires to mental and divine desires or needs.

As one learns to listen to and heed the inner urge of the

soul, the physical life ceases to overpower the Self. Instead, the Self becomes a center of creative power.

Being replaces doing. When the imaginative faculty is employed productively, action becomes easier, and all manifestations of one's creative mind proceed at a more rapid rate. In other words, it is easier and quicker to create when your mind is working for you instead of against you.

Thought is cause. The more enlightened one becomes the more thought is employed to achieve mighty results. Then the whole life is devoted to quickening one's soul growth. Then the process of enlightenment proceeds rapidly.

One is to harmonize with the environment. Through connectedness comes power. Love creates connectedness. The supreme development of connectedness is called unity consciousness; or union with the Godhead, or Christ consciousness, or cosmic consciousness, or Buddha consciousness, or en-LIGHT-enment.

All power comes from connectedness. The nature of physical life is separation, isolation, distance, and segmentation. The nature of the mental or spiritual life is connectedness, oneness, touching, and omniscience. The more enlightened one becomes the more one is connected with all life and all creation.

The one who rules the Self or the one who rules the world productively does not have a busy mind. A still mind that is a receptive mind is capable of ruling the Self and all of Mind. Only a still, receptive mind is capable of receiving all knowledge and all awareness.

A busy mind, with its myriad of limiting memory thoughts and sensory engrossment. remains mostly physical in its thinking. Such a one lives mostly in the physical brain and uses the mind very little.

The lesson is:
Release something, especially limitations every day be they mental, emotional, or physical. Discipline the mind to transform weakness into strengths and to become receptive.

Forty-nine

The Sage has no heart of his own
his heart is the heart of the people

To the good he is good
to the bad he is also good
until they become good
To the true he is truthful
to the false he is also truthful
until they become truthful

The Sage is in harmony with the world
through his heart he is universally connected
     with all humanity
People open their eyes and ears to him
to the Sage they are his children.

49

The wise one, the Sage, is aware of the universal connectedness of all beings. This wise reasoner realizes that as one aids others to betterment so the Self is also helped and aided.

The heart symbolizes and is the center of love and understanding. In fact, the Heart center or chakra has as its quality that of love and understanding. Love is fully necessary in order to build permanent and lasting understanding of connectedness. When one's love expands to include all beings, then the heart of Self becomes the heart of the people.

Jesus who became the Christ said, *"Whatever you wish men to do for you do likewise also for them; for this is the law and the prophets," (Matthew 7:12).* Jesus the Christ also said, *"You have heard it said, be kind to your friend, and hate your enemy. But I say to you, Love your enemies, bless anyone who curses you, do good to anyone who hates you and pray for those who carry you away by force and persecute you. So that you may become sons of your Father who is in heaven, who causes his sun to shine upon the good and the bad, and who pours down his rain upon the just and the unjust," (Matthew 5:43-45).*

It is very productive to be good to not only the good but also the bad because by this action one can grow in consciousness. The nature of reality is connectedness. As you think, so you become, is a Universal Truth. Therefore, it is important to be vigilant in causing one's thoughts to be productive and giving so that the Self may receive the greater learning in each situation.

As one practices more honesty, one becomes more honest. As one becomes more honest, one lives according to truth. As one lives according to truth, one lives in greater truth. As one lives in greater truth, one aligns with Universal Truth. As one aligns with Universal Truth, one lives in greater harmony and connectedness with all the Universe. The mind is capable of being used productively to cause one's consciousness to grow and one's awareness to expand.

Why be good to the bad and truthful to the false? Because such a one, in helping others to elevate their consciousness, does likewise in the process the same to and for the Self. It is one's practice ground.

When people know they are loved, they feel safe and secure. When people feel secure and safe, they are willing to open themselves up and listen. Those who are willing to open up and listen are capable of hearing the higher truth, the Universal Truth. Thus, to open their eyes and ears to the Sage is to receive wisdom and truth.

Since the Sage is more mature and evolved mentally as a soul, those less mature are as children for they have built less soul understandings. The ones who have gained and amassed soul understandings need to share and teach this to others. In order to receive from a greater soul one must give to lesser souls.

The enlightened being knows, perceives, and is aware he is connected to everything and everyone.

The Universal Laws operate everywhere and at all times. Every person is in essence an individual, an identity known as I AM. Therefore, each individual or I AM needs to know, perceive, and be aware of that connectedness with other I AM's.

All people have an inner urge from their own Real Self, which is I AM, to grow and mature as creators through connectedness consciousness until Self recognizes who he is through unity consciousness, which is also called union with God, union with the Godhead, or seeing God face to face.

Humbleness is the mark of a surrendered ego. An ego that is surrendered to I AM. The enlightened being's goal is not the accumulation of physical things. Rather the urge is to claim understanding of the spirit or High Self.

The confusion arises because while others create goals and desires the enlightened being creates ideals and fulfills the inner urge. Such a one speaks with authority because the truth of Self, of Mind, and of Creation is known.

Such a one continually creates a quality of infancy. The qualities of infancy are openness, absorption, curiosity, innocence, truth and Love.

Such a one continually learns, grows, expands consciousness, and is filled with greater Truth, Love, and LIGHT.

The wise soul, the intuitive thinker, has developed an expanded consciousness that is connected through the heart, and through love to all humanity.

When love is present, people do not fear. Therefore, it is easy for them to be open and to listen and to receive and perceive the truth.

The more enlightened one becomes, the more such a one perceives those less enlightened as children. The enlightened one, the Sage has more experience and understanding of Self, of Mind, of LIGHT, love and truth. Such a one lives the Universal Laws of Creation.

The Lesson is:
That which you do to others you also do to yourself.
All beings are connected. Expand one's love until it
is universal. Teach others the truths one has
learned.

Fifty

We come out into life
we go back into death
One in three are the followers of life
One in three are the followers of death
Those just passing through from life to death
also number one in three
But they all die in the end
Why is this so
because they live an intense life of attachment
to the changing, physical world

It is said that the one who excels in nourishing life
does not wear armor for battle
does not avoid rhinos or tigers in the wild
In such a one the rhino finds no place to thrust its
horn
the tiger finds no place to sink its claws
weapons have no place to pierce
Why is this so?
Because in such a one there is no space for death

The appearance or birth of a baby in our family or environment
indicates the appearance of a new life. It is the appearance of a
new life in the physical world because the soul or spirit now re-
siding in the baby's body had life prior to the present incarnation.
We, as souls, exist between lifetimes in the inner levels or inner
dimensions of Mind. More specifically souls exist between lifetimes in Subconscious, Universal Mind. The Subconscious Mind
is full of life.

Death seems to indicate the life or soul has disappeared
from the physical body. At the point of death the soul withdraws
its attention from the physical body. At death the life seems to
withdraw from the physical body. The soul or identity that in-
habited the physical body seems to disappear and goes back into
Subconscious Mind. Yet what we call life and death is in reality a
movement of consciousness, a shift in attention, a movement in
form, a stage of growth.

Between lifetimes the soul resides in Subconscious Mind
and assimilates the permanent learning and understanding gained
from the previous, most recent lifetime. When the learning of
the most recent lifetime has been integrated into the soul, it becomes permanent memory. Then the soul is ready to begin the
process of preparing for the next incarnation. A choice of land
area, time, and parents is needed. Yes, the soul does choose the
parents.

Fewer than one in ten people know the meaning of life
and live their life accordingly.

Three in ten or 30 percent live life with the intention of
learning and growing. They consciously desire to learn all their
lives. Yet they still do not fully know the meaning of life and how
to use the physical experience to the fullest to promote rapid soul
growth and spiritual development.

Three in ten or 30 percent of people live lives of total engrossment and entrapment in physical matter. They practice sen-

sory engrossment and die never realizing they are an eternal soul and not a temporary body.

Three in ten or 30 percent of the people go through life trying to do good and just experiencing life as it is without ever asking for the meaning of life. They just accept life as it is.

All three groups or 90 percent of the people go through life to death engrossed in the five physical senses and entrapped in the physical body.

Ten percent or less than one in 10 people know the meaning of life and are living it. They recognize that the essence of our being is LIGHT. They know that Truth and Love are the keys to understanding and knowing our essence of LIGHT. They discipline the mind to make it a very useful tool to come to know the Self. They realize that in order to know the Real Self and creation they must master the mind and come to be able to still the whole Mind and its myriad of thoughts.

The only way to go beyond death is to understand life. Life is a continuum of consciousness. Therefore, in order for one to gain eternal life one must develop the consciousness. One must master the mind in order to develop a continual consciousness and an unceasing awareness.

Of the one in ten who excels in nourishing life only one in ten of those seems willing to commit the Self to the quickening of soul growth. Fewer than one in one hundred are ready and willing to give the whole life and the whole Self and the whole mind to the relentless pursuit of knowing the Self.

The physical world is in a process of constant change although at least nine out of ten people view it as constant, or unchanging. Then these people grieve when change occurs in physical life. Our world is a bunch of molecules and atoms in constant motion. Therefore, our environment changes from one second to the next even if this change is not perceivable by the five senses.

To form attachments is to live in the illusion that things and life are unchanging. The truth is, the nature of the physical world and universe is change. An attachment is like an anchor that binds one or holds one in the same place. To be held in the same place is painful and unfulfilling since the world around us is in constant motion. The key then to fulfillment is to learn to cause there to be consistent forward motion in the consciousness of the Self and to ensure the growth and forward motion of the Self is greater than that of the surrounding world.

To regard the physical world as all there is to life indicates one will succumb to the temporariness of the physical world. People who make a living through physical activity alone end up becoming temporary because it is the nature of the physical world. A life lived for physical results only, with physical memory thoughts in the physical life, will cause the physical body to submit to the temporariness of physical time.

One who lives a life filled with the LIGHT of truth is mentally powerful and therefore does not need to protect the Self. Since thought is the cause of our life one whose thoughts dwell in truth never draw habits – symbolized by animals in this chapter – or uncontrolled change –symbolized by battle – to the Self.

Such a one controls and directs the changes and movement of consciousness within the Self. Such a one expands the consciousness beyond death for death is unconscious change. A director of one's mind and life is always conscious. Therefore, such a one never has times of unconsciousness.

The Lesson is:

Identify with life and Self as an eternal soul. Learn to discipline the mind in order to master consciousness.

Fifty-one

The Tao gives birth to all things
Te nourishes them
Nature forms them
Experience completes them

Therefore, all things respect the Tao
and honor Te
Respect for Tao
and honor of the Way
are not demanded of them
Yet always occur naturally

The Tao gives birth to them
and Te nourishes them
raises and develops them
stabilizes and matures them
comforts and protects them

To give birth without possessing
To give birth without expectation
To raise without controlling
This is called the mysterious power.

All forms and substance in Superconscious, Subconscious, and Conscious Minds arise from LIGHT. LIGHT was the first creation of the Creator when he said in the Bible, book of *Genesis,* Chapter 1, *"Let there be LIGHT."*

LIGHT then split into the receptive and aggressive principles of creation, yin and yang, Love and Truth. Thereby, forming the Superconscious Division of Mind. From these two Universal Principles are formed the other two Divisions of Mind which are Subconscious and Conscious Minds.

Everything created in Mind, all forms and all energy is nourished by the productive mind in alignment with LIGHT and the Creator's perfect, divine plan of Creation. All physical things, forms, or structures come from LIGHT and are nourished by a productive, LOVE, and Truth-filled mind.

Shapes and forms are affected and influenced by the environment and by nature. The physical life forms our conscious mind and brain as we grow and mature. Our conscious mind is shaped and formed in the first seven years of a lifetime. As we mature we choose our experiences. It is the choices we make that determine the outcome of our lives.

Thus all the many thousands of aspects of Self need to come to know the LIGHT of awareness and the value of a productive conscious mind that follows the inner urge. Each person has free choice and can therefore choose to live in the LIGHT of soul growth and understanding. Each person can also choose to ignore the inner Self thus creating pain and sorrow in the life.

One who lives in harmony with the Universal Laws of Mind, practices them. One who learns to be in perfect alignment with the Universal Laws and Truths finds the life's mission is accomplished in full.

Tao is the universal expression of Superconscious Mind. Te is the individual expression of Self and one's own mind. Sometimes Te is called virtue, or power, or integrity.

The Tao is the universe and Mind through which we live and move and have our being. Its energy is everywhere. Therefore, individuals honor and respect the Tao or Way when they have the least bit of harmony with Universal Law and Universal Truth. It is very important that each person, each individual learn to use their own mind because it is the most powerful and valuable tool each person can use to come to know the Self.

The Superconscious Mind gives birth to all the rest of Mind. It is one's own individual mind that gives one the opportunity to be nourished in soul growth and mental or spiritual development. The mind raises and develops the consciousness of the individual. It stabilizes and matures the Self. The mind gives one the way to develop the comforting quality, compassion, and truth which protect the Self.

The mind is to be used to develop the whole Self. The mind is the tool or vehicle to know the Self. The nature of the universe is change. The nature of Subconscious Mind is forward motion. Therefore, each must learn to cause continual forward motion in consciousness. To possess is to tie oneself down, to slow one's progress. To expect return from the one given to instead of from the universe restricts one's ability to receive from the universe. To raise or mature without controlling gives one the opportunity to expand one's perception. This is the secret of the Mind and Self that few know or practice.

In the *Book of Matthew* in the Bible, Jesus who became the Christ said, *"But seek ye first the Kingdom of Heaven and its righteousness and all else will be added unto you,"* (Matthew 6:33). Such a one finds the needs of Self are met and received from the Universe.

From the perfect seed idea of creation in Superconscious Mind comes the birth of all forms in the Subconscious and Conscious Mind. The physical world sometimes called the Conscious Mind Division of Mind gives form to substance.

It is through using the function of forms that we grow in awareness and understanding.

The Superconscious Mind is constantly giving life force unconditionally. It is always available. The one with an open mind learns to receive and use greater amounts of life force.

This unconditional and continuous giving of life force is a mysterious virtue. It is each individual's wonderful opportunity to have all the energy needed to achieve the goal and purpose in life.

The lesson is:

***Creation is continual.
Harmonize with creation by learning the
Universal Laws and Truths and align with
them. Learn to wield greater and greater
amounts of life force.
Techniques of conscious, disciplined breathing
will help one learn to
accomplish this.***

Fifty-two

The World has a maiden beginning
She became the Mother of the World
By knowing the Mother
one comes to understand her children
One who understands her children
is safely connected to the Mother
and creates a life of fulfillment

Close up the opening called the mouth
Close the gates of the senses
and you are never in trouble
Unblock the opening
meddle in affairs
and you are beyond all hope of saving

Seeing one's smallness is enlightenment
to softly yield is strength
use your Light of awareness to return home
The one of enlightenment
does not surrender to limitations
This is continual creation of the Hidden Immortal

To be a maiden is to be female. To be female is to be receptive. Receptivity then became the Mother of the World. The Mother of the World gives birth to all things. Know the Mother and thereby know the children. The children symbolize all aspects of Self. Aspects of Self are ways of thinking, attitudes, and the many facets of one's consciousness.

To know Self is the ideal of all spiritual aspirants and all students of the Mind. In order to know Self one must know all aspects of the Self. To know Self creates a life of fulfillment.

To close up the mouth and the senses is to still the mind. When the mind is still, there are no thoughts. When there are no thoughts, there are no words to speak. To speak in such a way as to argue or to get emotionally attached and engrossed in the experience of the senses, is to reduce or eliminate one's opportunity for enlightenment for a lifetime.

To perceive one's smallness in the overall scheme of creation is to maintain a humble ego. To softly yield is receptivity and also a humble ego. To have an over-inflated ego is to view yourself as bigger than you are which is false or wrong or inaccurate perception. Therefore, practice proper perspective in one's own Self evaluation. Remember every person is valuable. Not only you, but also every other person is very valuable. To trust one's perception is to act on needs and ideals while at the same time retaining a receptivity to situations and circumstances as they arise. This creates security.

To act, to initiate activity while retaining the receptive quality is to cause creation and learning for the Real Self, the immortal Self. To softly yield is the receptive quality. One who is truly and very much alive is continually creating. This is what creates immortal consciousness.

The lesson is:
Receptivity is to be used and maintained. From the receptivity develops greater enlightenment. Continually create soul learning.

Fifty-three

Were I to have even a little wisdom
I would follow the Great Way of Tao
and my only fear would be of going astray
The Great Way is simple and direct

Yet, people are distracted by side-paths
Their palaces are excessive in their splendor
They wear clothing of rich colors and fancy designs
They carry fine swords
They are excessive in food and drink
and possess more than they need
While their fields are overgrown with weeds
        and untilled
and their granaries are empty
This is called extravagant robbery
and robbery is not the Way of the Tao

53

The little wisdom that is required may be called listening to the inner urge of the Soul. The soul is always urging the conscious mind to move out of and beyond its engrossment in physical matter. This is the main road and the Way. The main road, the Great Way, is the road that leads to the greater LIGHT of awareness. It is the road of the Heart. It is the road of the productive use of the emotions. It is the road of Reasoning. It is the road of Intuition.

Straying from this road takes one down the path of engrossment in sensory stimuli, entrapment in physical existence and the physical body, darkness, death, sadness, sorrow, and pain.

It is easier to be disciplined in life, to practice self discipline – mental, emotional, and physical discipline than to be undisciplined.

The undisciplined person always fails to cause progress. The nature of the universe is forward motion. The one who moves forward faster than the universe experiences joy, bliss, and fulfillment. The one who fights change and forward motion experiences misery, dissatisfaction, and lack of fulfillment. Yet people allow themselves to be sidetracked by Maya, the sensory illusion that physical existence is permanent and the physical world is all there is to existence.

The court arrayed in splendor represents those people who give their whole physical lifetime to the pursuit and collection of physical objects and sensory gratification.

The first four verses of this chapter discuss what it is to have at least a little wisdom. To have a little wisdom is to make wise and productive choices every day and to teach this to others.

In order to make wise choices one must prioritize the life. The wise one, the one with great intelligence makes choices based upon what is lasting and permanent. The Tao or Way is lasting and permanent. Physical existence is temporary and changing. The Mind is simple and the Great Way is simple and direct. People get distracted by physical life. They forget what their purpose and assignment in life is and what they are here to accomplish. The side paths are anything that moves the attention away from building permanent understandings of Self and creation.

From this explanation of the proper use of the mind and attention in life, Chapter 53 goes on to give an example of the misuse of a physical life and physical existence.

Excessive palaces, clothing of rich colors, fine swords, excessive food and drink, and possession of more than is needed or used, are all examples of a person or people whose attention is misdirected to sensory gratification. Sensory gratification should never be the goal in life nor the top priority. The senses are to be used to gain and receive knowledge, insight, and understanding from the physical life that can then be reasoned with and added to the whole, permanent, and lasting Self which is the eternal soul in Subconscious Mind, the spirit in Superconscious Mind and I AM beyond Mind.

Fields untilled symbolize the mind that is being wasted and unused. Fields overgrown with weeds symbolize one who allows old doubts, fears, and unproductive thoughts to overrule and overpower all the value that could be produced in a life. It is the refusal to practice productive thoughts. Doubts and fears produce nothing productive and valuable in the life. Thought is cause and as we think so we become. Jesus referred to a similar subject in his parable of the sower and the seed in *Matthew* 13:1-13.

The way of the Tao and the way of the reasoner is to constantly add to one's awareness and understanding. The reasoner practices this in the world by constantly adding to the world and making the environment better than the day before.

The Way is simple and the Mind is simple. It is the brain and the five senses that interpret life as complicated. The brain and senses are physical. The Mind is mental. The five senses give us the mistaken impression that the perceiver is separate from all that is experienced.

The simple truth is distance and separation are an illusion produced by entrapment in a physical body with its attendant five senses and physical brain.

The Way of the Tao is connectedness through Life Force and consciousness. It is to be used to further the evolutionary progress of the soul.

The lesson is:

Be simple and direct.
Listen to the inner urge of the soul
to know the truth. The physical world
is a temporary schoolroom. Use it wisely
to progress in Light awareness
as a being of Light.

Fifty-four

What is firmly established in the Tao is not uprooted
What is firmly grasped in the Tao cannot slip away
as a result future generations will honor it
It will not slip away

When cultivated in the Self virtue becomes genuine
when cultivated in the family virtue overflows
when cultivated in the village virtue increases
when cultivated in the state virtue prospers
when cultivated in the world virtue is Universal

Thus, perceive persons through your own person
perceive the family through your family
perceive the village through your village
perceive the world through your world
How do I know what the world is like
through this understanding of what is within me.

54

When a lesson of creation is learned and made a part of Self it is stored in Subconscious Mind as a permanent and eternal part of one's soul. It is stored within the Self from incarnation to incarnation permanently. It is held within the Self even if the last lifetime is achieved or one is physically immortal. When the understanding of Mind and Self is correctly and completely grasped, the understanding is stored in Subconscious Mind as permanent memory.

Live according to Universal Law and Universal Truth and grow in peace, fulfillment, love, and understanding. The Understandings of Self will remain forever. One honors understandings every time they are used. Cultivate soul growth and spiritual development into an expanding consciousness and more and more aspects of Self are affected and benefitted.

As consciousness of the individual is expanded to include more of creation, such as family, village, state and world the greater goodness, kindness, love, joy and fulfillment will flow into the Self. As one aids others to uplift their consciousness then this also aids the Self. A family, village or state is made up of people. People symbolize aspects of Self when interpreted using dream symbology and the Universal Language of Mind. When virtue is cultivated to encompass the world then all aspects of Self have been mastered.

Therefore, still the mind and perceive all experience, all creation, and interaction as it is.

It is connected. It is not separate.

The Self is connected. Everything one does and thinks affects everyone and everything else. Therefore, perceive people through your own Self. You are not separate, isolated, alone, disjointed, or disconnected. Practice connectedness until a unity consciousness is achieved. How do I know the Universe is like this?

How do I know everything and everyone is connected?
I perceive,
my mind is expanded,
my heart is open,
I love. My consciousness grows.
Therefore, I am connected with the whole world.

The lesson is:

**The true nature of reality is universal connectedness.
Therefore, practice connectedness.**

Fifty-five

He who is filled with virtue
is similar to a newborn child
wasps do not sting him and serpents do not bite him
beasts do not seize him and birds of prey do not attack
him
his bones are flexible, his muscles are soft
yet his grip is firm
he has not known the union of male and female
yet his virility is strong
he screams all day
yet never becomes hoarse
so perfect is his harmony
He who knows harmony knows the eternal
He who knows the eternal is called enlightened
To increase life is a blessing
Things that are forced grow for a while then wither
away
To grow old while still in one's prime of life
is not in alignment with the Way
What is not in alignment with the Way
     comes to an early
     end.

When attention is always on the free flowing energy of giving and receiving, when intention is always to give freely without expectation of reward from the person given to, when love is given freely in the true spirit of connectedness, then all things are possible and all obstacles are overcome.

Doubts and fears will no longer control or override the true inner urge. Instead all creative energies – symbolized by snakes – will be used for the good of the whole. Everything done will be for the progression of mankind.

Habits symbolized by beasts will no longer control or limit the Self. Use all thoughts productively and all thoughts will be productive adding to the creation that is in place.

In the new idea or new manifestation symbolized by infancy, the form and structure one creates and uses is pliable, mobile, and flexible. This is because one's purpose is clear and powerful symbolized by a strong grip for hand symbolizes purpose.

Because one has the openness of infancy one is able to absorb all knowledge, wisdom, learning and enlightenment. Such a one immediately uses, plays with, teaches, and shares what has been learned.

Such a one exercises the will continuously without tiring. Such a one has no limits on bringing forth the mental images and, in fact, is continuous about this. Thus, such a one exists fully in the continuous harmony of forward motion and continual creation.

The continual forward motion of soul growth and the quickening of the spirit is harmony.

The qualities of the stage of growth known as infancy are openness, absorption, curiosity, innocence, trust and love. The one filled with virtue being similar to a newborn child displays these qualities. A baby is flexible mentally as well as physically. The infant is flexible mentally. The child opens to learning and absorbs and receives learning at all times. One who practices these qualities given does not create unproductive thoughts that then come back to cause the person grief or sorrow.

Hands symbolize purpose. One who is using the qualities of infancy has a strong desire to learn and has a purpose in doing so. One who uses the stage of infancy shares, expresses and gives everything he or she has, mentally, emotionally, and physically. One who practices the qualities of infancy is constantly improving the ability to reason.

To practice and use the stage of growth known as infancy is to live in harmony within Self and within nature. To know harmony is to know what is permanent, lasting and eternal. Understandings of Self and creation are permanent and lasting. Therefore, one should constantly strive to build a greater harmony within Self and through that with the world. One needs to strive to harmonize the conscious and subconscious minds and attune them to superconscious mind. In this way one can increase life for life is motion. To increase life is to cause a quickening of one's forward motion as a soul.

To use force is to affect something physically only. Anything lasting and permanent must be built or manifested mentally, emotionally, and physically. Anything that is physical only is temporary for it is the nature of physical existence. To grow old while still in one's prime is to forget to continue to learn and grow in every situation. What is not in alignment with the Way is not mental, emotional, and physical. It is mostly physical.

The Subconscious Mind is for forward motion which is an adding to one's storehouse of permanent understandings of creation and the Universal Laws governing creation.

He who hurries always loses time. An out of control, rushing mind makes mistakes, uses poor judgements, and forgets the location of important objects. The mind needs to be stilled and quieted in order to be brought under the direction and use of the thinker.

Most people restrict their use of prana or life force. The

mind and breath must be used together and in harmony to produce enlightenment. Most people restrict their breathing. Most people do not even know how to breath correctly. Thus, they receive little prana.

People need to learn how to breathe like a newborn baby. It is the natural life breath. The energy is to be given and then received freely and with no restriction. Then one always has enough.

The way of the Tao which is OM, the vibration of creation, is the free movement of the Aggressive and Receptive Principles of Creation. This is the inbreath and the outbreath of God. Such creation is continual and therefore eternal.

The lesson is:

Remember to be like a child and learn every day. Always cause increase and add to yourself and your world. This is the hallmark of a reasoner.

Fifty-six

Those who know do not talk
Those who talk do not know
Seal the opening of your mouth
close the gate of the senses
dull your sharpness
simplify your tangled thoughts
soften your glare
be connected with the dust of the world
This is called the Secret Union

Thus, one who knows this secret
is not affected by attachment
is not practicing avoidance
is not controlled by profit
is not affected by loss
is not affected by honor
is not touched by disgrace
Such a one is beyond the physical world temporariness
and exists in the Highest state of consciousness

As *Ecclesiastes 1:2* in the Bible says, *"Vanity of vanities; all is vanity."* Vanity is the misuse of the conscious ego. The productive use of the ego is motivation. The ego is your motivator. A dishonest conscious ego will motivate one to sensory engrossment. A productive honest ego will motivate one to reason.

Sensory engrossment means allowing one's senses to determine one's decisions in life. Sensory experiences are temporary by their very nature. Therefore, one who invests their life's energies in temporary experiences finds over time there is little added to the soul in terms of LIGHT, Love, Truth, and permanent understandings.

The one who is correctly motivated by their ego to pursue and master the eternal truths of the universe and creation, receives a fulfillment beyond compare. For that which is permanent and lasting is added to the soul. The permanent learning termed understandings that are added to the soul are fulfillment in the truest sense of the word which is to fill full.

One who is secure within Self and who has a productive forward motion producing conscious mind ego does not have to talk and convince others of the accomplishment of Self. Such a one may talk of these; however, from a point of giving encouragement and vision to others. Those who talk only for the purpose of impressing others have yet to build the security in Self that comes from the repeated success of learning and applying the Universal Laws of Creation.

Oneness of Self with all of creation comes first from stilling the mind, because at first the mind is scattered. The mind thoughts are scattered due to the ego being attracted to a multitude of sensory stimuli. This produces the pain and sorrow of disconnectedness.

Next the Self, desiring more fulfillment in life, seeks a teacher in order to be taught about the mind and Self. Then one learns concentration in order to still the mind. As the mind is stilled the alignment of conscious and subconscious minds occurs. Then is the mind free to expand and thus gains connectedness with other minds of like interest.

Then mind continues in this process of connecting with more and more minds and more of nature and more of creation until connectedness evolves to a unity consciousness. This is the secret union of the primary or main Self and mind with Universal Mind and Creator. It is a mystery until one experiences the Union. The use of the word union does not indicate dissolvement or loss of individuality. Instead the Real Self gains a true understanding of individuality. The Real Self gains a true understanding of Self and comes into a mental and spiritual maturity of Self as I AM. To know I AM is to know individual-identity as a Creator being filled with LIGHT.

The one who has achieved this state of en-LIGHT-enment understands eternity, lives in the present moment and is secure in Self's full connection with Creator which banishes the illusion of distance and therefore physical time.

The temporary states and sensory experiences of physical life no longer distract such a one from the connected consciousness of the Divine Self. This union with the Godhead, embracing the Creator and unity consciousness, is the highest state of consciousness.

The Bhagavad Gita, Chapter 8 says, *"Close tightly those gates of the body, which men call the avenue of the senses. Concentrate the mind on the inner Self."* This is almost exactly what the Tao Te Ching says in the statement, *"close the gate of the senses."*

The Bhagavad Gita goes on to say, *"Concentrate thy mind upon thine inner Self. Let thine 'I' dwell in full strength, within its abode, not seeking to move outward. Stand firm, fortified by the Yogi power, and repeat in The Silence, the mystic syllable 'AUM', the symbol of My being as Creator, Preserver, and Transformer, according to the letters or sounds thereof. Then, faithful to this, when thou quittest thy mortal frame, with thy thoughts fixed upon Me, shalt thou pass on to the Path of Supreme Bliss."* This Supreme Bliss referred to in the Bhagavad Gita is the same as the Mysterious or Secret union given in the Tao. The

Supreme Bliss occurs from achieving the secret union. This union is the alignment of Conscious and Subconscious Minds and then attunement of both to Superconscious Mind. This then leads to union with I AM. One who has gained Union with the Godhead or I AM knows the real mystery of Self and Creation.

Attachment, avoidance, profit, loss, honor and disgrace are all functions or reactions to physical and emotional life. They are of the lower levels of Mind.

The one who has gained union exists in Superconscious Mind with full awareness and knowing of Self. In this there is no separation. In this, all is given and all is received. All is shared and all is learned.

An individual who has achieved this level of awareness has gone beyond the illusion of the temporary and separate, and lives in the eternal now of full consciousness.

The lesson is:

Constantly strive for full connectedness of consciousness. Gain superconscious awareness.

Fifty-seven

To govern the state have straight forward direction of
      action
to fight a war have surprise tactics and deceitful action
to gain all under heaven, stop trying to control
      the action
How do I know this works
the more laws and prohibitions there are
the poorer the people become
the more sharp weapons
the more darkness and confusion in the state
the more scheming and cleverness
the more strange things occur
the more fine treasure abounds
the more numerous are thieves and robbers

Thus, the Sage, the Holy One says
I practice expectant non-action
and the people naturally transform themselves
I have a still mind
and the people naturally correct themselves
I do not interfere with affairs
and the people naturally become prosperous
I practice desirelessness
and the people naturally create the good and simple
      life

57

Goals are mental images usually of physical things one wants to achieve. A country or state is a physical entity, place or thing. To govern something physical like a country one needs to have a directed mind that then directs the action.

Because war is basically a process of destroying, the destroyer finds that in order to succeed deceit must be undertaken because most people do not want to be destroyed nor do they desire to destroy one another.

Both examples are attempts to control the physical life and the physical environment, and to control the physical life of others. However, to gain all under Heaven is to come to know the whole Self and the whole Mind – mental, emotional, and physical. To try to control the action, to try to control anything is of the nature of attachment and will only cause one to be more physically engrossed in physical experience.

To gain the Universe or all of Mind one has no goals at all because goals of their very nature are physical. To gain the Universe, ideals replace goals. Ideals are of the nature of ideas.

An ideal is what one wants to become.
A goal is what one wants to do.

Therefore, in order to gain the Universe or the whole of Mind and all of consciousness one must focus all the thoughts and attention on enlightenment. Enlightenment is the ideal of all who strive to know the Self.

The more one lives in harmony with Universal Laws the more abundant and prosperous one becomes.

One who lives according to Universal Laws is at peace with Self. There is no conflict therefore there is no need to wage war.

One who masters Self, masters the universe, because thought is cause.

Physical laws are laws of restriction. Universal Laws are laws of expansion. Physical laws are temporary. Mental or Uni-

199

versal Laws are permanent and eternal. This is why small government is good government.

When laws or rules replace goodness, love, and kindness, then people become devious instead of truthful, clever instead of wise, and ingenious instead of enlightened.

The more one lives by rules and regulations the more movement away from Universal Law and Universal Truth occurs.

Steal from others and you steal from Self. Steal from Self and you steal from others. What you do to yourself you do to others. What you do to others you do to yourself.

Always offer your love, kindness, goodness, and truth. Let people make their own decisions. They learn from their actions when they are taught the Universal Truths.

When one is at peace those around them experience more peace. When people begin to experience peace they are naturally more honest. Give people a place and an opportunity to succeed. Give encouragement and they will succeed. This is the history of the great country of the United States of America. As long as the government stays out of the way people prosper. When there is much government interference, it destroys the backbone of this country which is free enterprise and capitalism.

Free enterprise and the freedoms guaranteed in the *United States Constitution* have worked for this country and any other place they have been used. Communism and Socialism practiced in countries has always failed because they strive to control and restrict people.

Give the people their freedom and they become rich, prosperous, and abundant.

Gautama the Buddha said, *"Attachment to desire is the cause of all pain and suffering."* This was given in his great Four Noble Truths and Eight Fold Path or Way. Therefore, go beyond temporary physical desires to eternal spiritual needs for soul growth, spiritual development, enlightenment, and the development of the Mind.

The mind is simple because it is based on connectedness. Physical life is complicated because it is based on the false premise of separateness. Seen through the five senses, life appears to be segmented, separated, fragmented, disjointed, and isolated.

Viewed from the Higher Mind all life is perceived as a unity. All beings are to come to be connected in consciousness.

This is the good and simple life. This is the great life of a master Creator.

This wise one, the Sage, practices expectant non-action which is receptivity. The drawing power of receptivity can aid people to transform their lives and their very Self.

A still mind has a calming and peaceful effect on all those around the Self. Because the Sage gives the people room to create they become prosperous – mentally, emotionally, and physically.

The lesson is:

Create a strong mental image of who and what one desires to become. Practice receptivity in order to receive the full manifestation of the ideal of enlightenment into the Self.

Fifty-eight

When the government is non-invasive
the people are open and simple
When the government is invasive
the people become needy and cunning

Disaster depends on good fortune
Good fortune has disaster concealed
Who knows what Heaven sends
or what the future holds

When there is no fixed rightness
rightness turns into wrong
good turns into evil
the people have been confused
for a long time

Thus, the Sage has a sharpness that does not injure
has a point that does not hurt
is straight forward yet is not severe
is illumined yet does not blind

When living in a state of love and LIGHT few rules or laws of conduct are needed. When the government is non-invasive, the people can succeed by being simple and open. When the government is invasive, the people try to succeed by other means.

When control is established only by rules and laws people seek to circumvent those rules because they restrict their freedom and create poverty. Hence, in dictatorships there exists a heavy black market as an attempt at free enterprise. When the government is controlling, the people become cunning in seeking to find ways to have control of their lives and to fulfill their needs.

When people exist and live according to love and LIGHT, life is simple for everyone is connected. Everyone is a good neighbor to everyone else. Everyone helps each other because everyone loves each other.

What most people refer to as happiness or good fortune, is a fleeting, temporary occurrence. One can be happy one day and experience disaster the next.

Love for the Creator and Creation is lasting. The fulfillment of soul growth and permanent understandings is lasting and eternal. The LIGHT added to the whole Self is eternal.

As long as the individual is under the control of the pairs of opposites which are the extremes of physical existence, there will continue to be misery. Examples of these extremes or pairs of opposites expressed in physical existence are cold and hot, black and white, up and down, good and bad, right and wrong, happy and sad.

Until one is taught Universal Truths and Universal Laws, he or she will sway from honesty over time for the pull of existence will entrap the Self. The engrossed Self becomes more and more entrapped until the choice is made to end the suffering.

As long as one lives under the pairs of opposites there is confusion in the mind. The physical senses give the illusion of separateness.

The Sage, the enlightened being, is able to communicate effectively and in such a way that those desiring to learn and progress in soul awareness can receive the Universal Truth. The voice of the Sage is used to uplift other's consciousness and fill them with LIGHT and love.

The enlightened master of the mind can be exact and to the point in sharing and teaching Universal Laws and Truths. The truths go in and the people receive them as beneficial. Able to direct his power to illumine and teach others such a one is filled with LIGHT and love that benefits all who are willing to receive.

The enlightened one aids others to see the greater LIGHT of truth and awareness without overpowering others with the truth.

The lesson is:

Give freely. Share the learning, knowledge, wisdom, and awareness.

Fifty-nine

In directing people and serving Heaven
nothing surpasses thriftiness and economy
Economy means to surrender and be receptive
to the Divine Plan

To surrender and be receptive to the Divine Plan
means accumulating understandings
Accumulating understandings of Self and creation
means infinite capacity
Infinite capacity means one can be a ruler
Using the Mother quality of receptivity and
nourishing works well for a long time
This is called having deep roots and a solid trunk

It is the Way of long life and eternal awareness

People, in Holy Books and in your night dreams, symbolize aspects of Self. Heaven symbolizes Superconscious Mind.

Economy means to accomplish efficiently and without waste. So whether one is directing a country or directing oneself it is important to be efficient, productive, and without waste.

To use every situation to the fullest for soul growth is to surrender to the Divine Plan of Creation.

To accumulate virtue is to build permanent understandings of Self and Creation thus furthering one's enlightenment. Everyone has the same amount of seconds, minutes, and hours in a day. The same amount of days in a year. The years come and go. The wise live the life for what is lasting and eternal. This is economy. Economy is to waste nothing and to use every opportunity to advance one's consciousness.

The Divine or Perfect Plan of Creation, the blueprint for each individual being, is held in Superconscious Mind. To live this plan, this blueprint, is to achieve the infinite possibility of becoming an enlightened being, a creator. Jesus the Christ said, *"Greater things than I do, you shall do also, for I go to the Father in Heaven."*

We have had over 2000 years of time and incarnations to perfect and develop ourselves since the time that Jesus of Nazareth walked the Earth in Palestine. Many have evolved in that length of time. Now is the time and possibility for many Christs and many Buddhas to come forth from humanity. Jesus the Christ stated that there would be many more Christs or enlightened beings that would develop and come forth to lead humanity in the Bible book of *John 14:12*, *"Truly, truly I say to you, He who believes in me shall do the works which I do; and even greater than these things he shall do, because I am going to my Father."*

The Mother Principle of ruling is the Receptive Principle of Creation. It is the nurturing quality. It nourishes life.

One who is receptive and thus receives new learning is able to expand one's consciousness rapidly. This quality includes truth, love and the joy of living. These qualities can nurture any creation. These qualities form a strong, solid foundation for growth and expansion of consciousness. From this firm foundation, created and maintained by receptivity, can come rapid growth and expansion of consciousness. This, in turn, makes possible the effective exercising of the Aggressive Principle of Creation. Receptivity is a strong foundation from which to build any creation.

Life is directed motion. A long life and eternal awareness are produced by one who continually strives to add to creation and expand perception which evolves to omniscient awareness which is the awareness of one who knows.

What good is eternal life without consciousness? The higher and more expansive one's consciousness the greater and more alive one is and the more one lives in eternal consciousness. Eternal life is unbroken or continual consciousness.

The lesson is:

The greatest economy for a day, a week, a month, a year, or a century is to follow one's inner urge and live it thereby gaining enlightenment.

Sixty

Ruling a large state
is like cooking a small fish
Govern the world in accord with the Tao
and evil spirits and dark thoughts will express no power
not only will the evil spirits and dark thoughts
    have no power
but their power can no longer harm the people
Not only will it do no harm to others
but the Sage also does the people no harm
When neither harms the people
Their virtue will be combined, returned
and restored

60

Fish symbolize spiritual awareness when interpreted in the Universal Language of Mind. Fire can hurt you yet when used with receptivity, care and reasoning, it is a wonderful tool for preparing food. Food symbolizes knowledge for just as physical food nourishes our physical body, so does spiritual food feed the soul or subconscious mind. Spiritual food is knowledge and interiorized learning of the secrets of creation.

To rule a country or to rule the 144,000 aspects of Self one must gain knowledge of Self and the interconnectedness of all creation. This requires receptivity, care and reasoning.

Approach the universe receptively in order to make correct choices of movement forward which is the aggressive quality of creation. Evil is intentionally choosing unproductive thoughts and actions. Evil is overcome and transcended by those who interiorize, live, and apply the Receptive and Aggressive Principles of Creation.

Unproductive thoughts and unproductive actions that proceed from them have the power to destroy and are destructive. Those who apply the Receptive and Aggressive Principles of Creation in balance are productive and creative while aiding more and more people.

The Sage, the enlightened being, is protected by living the Tao, the Perfect Plan of Creation held in Superconscious Mind the balance of Receptive and Aggressive Principles. Such a one creates heaven on earth.

This goodness that comes from a balance of the Aggressive and Receptive Principles of Creation aids, helps and adds to all. It uplifts all of creation and everyone in the immediate environment just as a well cooked fish nourishes those who partake of its nutrition.

Cooking a small fish is seen as simple because no preparation is needed. Put the whole fish in the pan and cook it. To rule effectively, whether a state or one's state of mind, one must remember that mind is simple. Therefore, the thinker stills the mind thereby simplifying the thoughts. The Tao is simple. It is the conscious mind, the five senses and the brain that make life complicated by suffering under the illusion of Maya, which is the illusion that everything is separate and that the physical life is permanent.

When the mind is stilled and quieted one's own thoughts no longer harm the Self. Instead one lives in harmony with all of Mind and all the Universal Laws.

The lesson is:

Make the life simple instead of complicated.
This is accomplished by living in harmony
with all of creation.

Sixty-one

A great state is like the lower part of a river
it is the receiving place of everything flowing into it
it is the female of the world
Through stillness the female conquers the male
In order to be still
she needs to be lower
The great state that is lower
can accordingly win over the smaller states
The small state that is lower
can accordingly win over the great state
Some lower themselves to govern
Some lower themselves to be governed

The great state's only desire
is to unite and lead others
The small state's only desire
is to devote itself to the service of the people
So in order for both to achieve their desires
The great state needs to be lower

When rain falls from the sky it travels from the hills to the valley in creeks, ditches, and streams. These streams then converge into rivers because of gravity. All water flows to the low land.

Creative energy and mind substance in like fashion flow to a great country and to a great person.

Great minds of great people working together and in harmony with a common ideal and a common vision are required in order to produce a great country.

The female which represents the receptive quality overcomes the male or aggressive quality by using a still mind. A still mind can receive the treasures of the universe. The still mind has drawing power. The aggressive mind can initiate action and can attempt to move forward but lacks drawing power.

One lies low in stillness so that any destructive action will pass over leaving Self unharmed. After the destructive motion of undirected or visionless energy and substance passes over, the receptive ones rise to nurture a new creation into existence.

Therefore, a large state when receptive to a smaller state will draw the smaller state into it. A small country that is receptive to a large country may draw the larger country into its ideas and vision of the future.

The future is won through ideas – for ideas are the creative mechanism. Thought is cause. This is a Universal Truth. Creativity comes from imaged thoughts.

Great ideas change the world permanently, and for the better. Aggressive force destroys the opportunity for growth and the forward march of progress.

To yield is to surrender. To surrender Self is to surrender one's Conscious Mind ego. To surrender one's conscious ego one must have love first and truth second although both are needed. To surrender is to sacrifice one's ego. To sacrifice is to make sacred.

Give service to others and expand beyond the small conscious ego to I AM which is more expansive than all of Mind which includes Conscious, Subconscious and Superconscious Minds.

To conquer or master Self, one needs to master all the thousands of aspects of Self. To master all aspects of Self, one must surrender the conscious mind to the High Self mind. One must practice love and truth. To practice love and truth, one must be willing to be receptive and receive.

A great state which symbolizes all aspects of the Self needs to be brought under the power of the Real Self.

Always strive to bring more aspects of Self into the field of one's awareness and use.

Each person needs to serve and give service to something greater than itself. Each person needs to give to others. Each person needs to become a student and teacher of the good, the true, and the love. This is the highest service.

Through mental discipline, truth, love, vision, and the aggressive and receptive qualities one achieves what has been imagined or imaged.

It is good and productive for all great people, all spiritual people, and all disciplined aspects of Self to be receptive and enjoy the power, goodness, and fulfillment of the drawing power. This is the power to draw all aspects or any aspect of creation into the Self.

Consider the great state as I AM or the whole Self. Consider the small state as the small ego or honest conscious mind and ego. I AM desires to direct all aspects of Self and cause them to function together. The disciplined, honest conscious ego desires to know Self and to know I AM.

Therefore, the awareness of I AM must be brought into the lower, conscious awareness. This requires a still and receptive mind.

The lesson is:
Come to know the power of receptivity.

213

Sixty-two

The Tao is the storehouse of creation
it is the treasure of the good man
and protection for the bad
With beautiful words one may sell
with honest conduct one can accomplish even more
Why should we reject people who are bad

Thus, when emperors are crowned
or the three ministers of state installed
though they may have large jade discs
and be preceded by teams of four horses
it is not as good as sitting in stillness
and offering the Tao
What was the reason the ancients
valued the Tao so highly
Did they not say
     seek and you will find
     sin and you will be forgiven
Therefore, knowing the Tao in the stillness
is the greatest treasure in the World

The Tao is the storehouse of creation because from the Aggressive and Receptive Principles of Superconscious Mind come all the myriads of forms, things, and structures we experience with the five senses in the physical world.

Self is individual and is known as I AM. I AM in its movement through the divisions of Mind from Superconscious to Subconscious Mind takes on the appearance of many separate parts or aspects of Self. It is the divine, creative LIGHT from the creator that becomes life force in Superconscious Mind that then provides life force for all of Mind.

Honesty aligns with truth and truth aligns with Universal Truth. When honesty is expressed in one's conduct then the truth manifests in one's actions. Thus ideal, purpose, and activity come to be in alignment and work together in order for the individual to fulfill the assignment of a lifetime. This is why with honest conduct one can accomplish so much.

The one who lives by truth and comes to understand Universal Truth lives more and more in the LIGHT. Such a one more and more is filled with and permeated with LIGHT. Such a one is filled with Love and Truth which together are LIGHT. Such a being understands the connectedness of the Universe. The connectedness in LIGHT.

Connectedness in LIGHT is the greatest treasure. The good thinker identifies this treasure because through the disciplined use of mind the permanent and true reality is revealed. Thus, the advancement of the soul is permanent and lasting while jade, gold, and jewels are temporary and fleeting.

The Superconscious Mind continually provides life force to all of mind and everyone. Therefore, to be in alignment with this we are not to practice avoidance. Instead we are to embrace the learning in everything we draw to ourselves through the Law of Karma and the Law of Cause and Effect. We are to learn the lesson that aligns with Universal Truth and Universal Law and move forward to the next higher stage of awareness.

The phrase when the emperor is crowned symbolizes your own success in physical life. It indicates the thinker has learned he is the creator of his life. It shows control of the power to create. The crown symbolizes authority. The crown chakra is the chakra that utilizes and transforms the highest creative energies available to each individual and all mankind.

The three ministers of state represent the Conscious, Subconscious and Superconscious Minds and therefore indicate the one who is gaining mastery over the whole Self and the whole Mind. It may also be compared to the Father, Son, and Holy Spirit of the Bible. No physical treasures are as valuable as having a still mind for by the still mind is the real Self known.

Physical objects will not bring mastery of consciousness. The aggressive quality alone will not bring en-LIGHT-enment. One enters the Superconscious Mind receptively. One receives the consciousness of Superconscious Mind receptively. You cannot force your way into Superconscious Mind for Superconscious Mind is not separate nor apart from you. Superconscious Mind surrounds us as infinite consciousness at all times.

Therefore, still the mind and know the High consciousness of the Self that is between the thoughts. Offer giving and receiving. Offer life force from Superconscious Mind. Offer LIGHT.

LIGHT which is awareness, banishes all darkness of fear, doubt, and destructiveness. LIGHT gives fulfillment, peace, joy, and bliss. This is why the ancients valued the Tao. LIGHT gives love and truth. Therefore, LIGHT gives power.

The LIGHT of awareness forgives all sins because awareness overcomes ignorance. LIGHT illumines so that what is sought is perceivable.

The greatest treasure of the universe is the LIGHT of awareness that proceeds from the Creator. The LIGHT is perceived by the still mind. The Tao is known in the still mind. This is the most valuable treasure.

This chapter of the Tao says, *"seek and you will find, sin and you will be forgiven."* This is very similar to the instructions of Jesus the Christ as given in *Matthew 7:7-8, "Ask, and it shall be given to you; seek, and you shall find; knock and it shall be opened to you. For whoever asks, receives; and he who seeks, finds; and to him who knocks, the door is opened."* And also in *Matthew 6:14-15, "For if you forgive men their faults, your Father in heaven will also forgive you. But if you do not forgive men, neither will your Father forgive even your faults."*

Therefore, the Bible in this case gives an explanation of the value of seeking and how to be forgiven. To read, study, and come to understand the Tao is to end all seeking, gain the full forgiveness, and to know the Self. For this the still mind is essential.

The lesson is:

Practice and come to know the still mind then use the still mind to open the door to all of Mind and thereby come to know the Self.

Sixty-three

Practice expectant non-action

effort without doing

discover taste in the tasteless

large or small many or few

repay hatred with love and truth

plan for the difficult while it is still easy

take action on the large while it is small

the most difficult tasks in the world begin easy

the greatest achievements in the world begin small

Therefore, the Sage stays with his daily tasks

     and thus accomplishes great things

beware of those who promise a quick and easy way

taking things lightly creates difficulties

because the Sage never avoids difficulties

He never experiences difficulties in the end

Receptivity is expectant non-action. Receptivity affords one the opportunity to draw to the Self situations, circumstances, and conditions necessary for one's learning and growth. Through the receptive quality, the thinker is able to notice and be aware of the forms and opportunities created in the life by one's thoughts.

The engrossed, matter-soaked person works for the purpose of doing, for a physical goal to get a job done.

The enlightened being or person does activity with purpose towards an ideal of becoming. The enlightened person works in order to become what he has imagined himself becoming.

Since the time in the past of Atlantis when humanity became entrapped in physical, animal man bodies, soul growth and permanent understandings have been accomplished through and by activity. Before entrapment in a physical body each individual learned and gained permanent or everlasting understandings and soul growth through observation or the process of observation.

Entrapment was the process whereby each individual soul became engrossed in the observation of animal man, the early form that would become human. The souls then misused and mentally controlled the animal man bodies and thus created a Karmic debt that could only be paid by changing the method of learning and gaining soul understandings from observation to direct physical participation called activity.

The one who works without doing is once again practicing learning through observation. Even though such a one may be engaged in activity the mind is objectively observing the experience and adding the learning in the experience to one's soul or subconscious mind.

By stilling the mind one is able to go beyond sensory experience to perceive directly with the mind. Thus, one is able to experience higher energies, more refined vibrations than are normally available to the senses. From this heightened, thrill of experience, a new life ensues.

Learn to identify all aspects of creation. One who gives full attention to any experience while maintaining a still and quiet mind enjoys the whole of creation. The person relying only upon the five senses for knowledge receives less than ten percent of the total experience. In this way valuable knowledge, learning and understanding is missed. To discover taste in the tasteless, one must go beyond the senses to perceive directly with the mind.

Always practice love because love connects. Bitterness and hatred divide and separate causing isolation, pain, loneliness, and despair. Connectedness creates purpose for living, joy, fulfillment, bliss, and the real happiness.

The mind is simple in that all is connected. The false illusion of the physical senses is that all is separate, disconnected and unrelated. Gautama the Buddha, the enlightened one said, *"Hatred can never put an end to hatred, love alone can. This is the unalterable law,"* (Dharmapada 1:6).

Little things are the essence of Creation for little or small things are the foundation of the world. Master the little things and achieve great things. It is the little thoughts one thinks and actions one takes each day that lead to large and great achievements. Difficult tasks or goals or activities are achieved by one act at a time, one step at a time. Therefore, great acts are made up of small deeds. No one ever became enlightened for only one act or deed. That one act or deed was but the culmination process of years and eons and lifetimes of directed struggle, effort, and activity to master the laws of the universe, the Universal Laws.

The one with en-LIGHT-enment achieves steps of creation every day. She moves forward in consciousness constantly and consistently and therefore achieves greatness.

Cause your words and thoughts to match. Cause your words, actions and thoughts to align.

Beware the person who pretends to be one thing outwardly and is something else inside in their thoughts. Therefore, view each action, thought, and emotion with equal importance. Give each attention daily.

Cease to practice avoidance. There is no learning in avoidance. Give full attention to whatever presents itself in the environment. Difficulties are not to be avoided anymore than good times are to be avoided. Experience is to be used for the soul growth and spiritual development of the Self. Receive experiences into the Self in order to learn. Because of this, the enlightened being never experiences difficulties. Instead he gives and receives. By this method one does not create difficulties in the life. Instead one experiences life with the mind and learns the lessons of life and creation rapidly.

The lesson is:

Learn to receive the most from each experience.
Take action each day on goals and ideals.
Never avoid the Karmic Lesson
pursue diligently the goal of enlightenment.

Sixty-four

It is easy to have a still mind in times of peace
it is easy to plan for before it manifests
it is easy to dissolve while still fragile
it is easy to dispense while still small
Act before things manifest in physical life
bring order before it returns to chaos
A tree as large as the arm's embrace grows from a small seed
A great terrace nine layers high starts from a basketful of dirt
A journey of one thousand miles begins with a single step
but to act is to fail
to control is to lose

Therefore, the Sage does not act
Thus he does not fail
he does not control
Thus he does not lose
When people pursue a goal
they usually fail when nearing completion
Therefore, giving as much caring attention
near the completion as at the beginning
creates an end to failure

Therefore, the Sage desires not to desire
and does not value hard to obtain physical objects
He learns what no one else learns
He returns to what others pass by
in order to help all beings to know the Self
Yet, he accomplishes this without interfering

64

Thought is cause. Thought is the cause of physical events. Thought is the cause of events that impact our lives. Thought is the point of control and power. By the time a thought moves into one's physical life one is experiencing the effects.

In order to change the course of events before they occur or are made manifest in our lives, it is necessary that we change the thoughts that will or are causing the event, circumstance, or situation.

The causal thought of your life as an adult is you. Why are you reading these words now, at this place, at this point in time? You are reading these words because of a choice you have made. Life is a series of choices and decisions. Thus you create your life with your creative or habitual thoughts and the decisions made based upon those thoughts.

Trouble is overcome before it starts by changing one's thoughts. Change your thoughts and you change your attitudes. Change limiting thoughts and attitudes and change your world because you expand your consciousness beyond previously held limitations.

The one who holds a still mind experiences no confusion. A thinker with a disciplined mind, a still and quiet mind is never confused. Therefore, there is order. When there is order things are understood. All is simple. Mind is simple because it is all connected.

All creations begin as a seed idea. The mighty oak tree begins as an acorn. Inside that acorn is the living blueprint for an oak tree. All things great and small in your life began and came from a living seed idea or thought.

All goals, all dreams, all ideals, and creations began as a creative thought in someone's mind.

A journey of one thousand miles begins with a single step. The point is that great accomplishments are achieved by repeated choice.

To function mainly or solely from activity or action is to fail because the point of power is the point of cause which is thought, not the activity or action. To try to control anything is to limit one's own consciousness.

All is created from thought. Thought is the substance from which our dreams are made. Therefore, instead of control; create, use and build, improve and add to what is within and around the Self.

To depend solely on action to achieve your desires is pure folly. The body must co-operate with the mind. The mind needs to form a clear thought that mind substance can form around in order to form the object of your desire.

The one who is greedy lives in and operates from fear. Think the thought and co-operate with the thought as it manifests and becomes a part of your outward life. Desires come to the Sage for he draws the manifested thought form to the Self consciously and with awareness. There is no separation. There is no distance. The one who depends on action only to achieve his goals finds there is a gulf or chasm separating him from the object of desire. This makes it hard and difficult to achieve. The easy way is to use your mind.

People often fail when they are on the verge of success because they have low Self esteem. They therefore fail to connect themselves with – or fail to admit their connectedness with – the more expansive life about to manifest as the object of their desire.

Therefore, the en-LIGHT-ened being thinks thoughts of

LIGHT, Love, Truth, joy, fulfillment, connectedness and expansiveness. And so this is what she creates in the life. This in turn benefits the lives of others who are willing to receive the LIGHT.

Attachment to desires keeps the Self engrossed in physical experiences. The Sage learns and builds permanent understandings of Self and creation. The average person does not even know what these are.

The lesson is:

The secret to successful creation is image, imagine, or visualize a clear, mental picture of what one desires to create, receive or manifest in the life.

Initiate physical activity on this imaged desire or need every day. Continue acting on this ideal or goal until it is fully manifested in one's life. Cooperate with others in fulfilling your needs. This is natural connectedness.

Sixty-five

The ancient masters who practiced the Way
did not try to make the people smarter
but instead intended for them to be simple hearted
What makes the people hard to rule
is outer intellectual knowledge
to rule the state with intellectual knowledge
is to rob the state
to rule state without intellectual knowledge
brings blessings to the state
One who understands these two
understands the Universal Principle
to understand the Universal Principle
is called hidden power
Hidden power goes deep and far
it leads all things to return to the source
until it reaches complete connectedness

In past times the secrets of creation were hidden from the masses of people and given only to the select few. These select few were either from the royal houses such as the Pharaohs in Egypt or they were especially spiritual people who gave their whole life's energies and work to the temple and its studies. They took an oath, under penalty of death, never to reveal these Universal Truths and secret Universal Laws of Creation to the uninitiated.

In those ancient times mankind as a whole was not nearly so evolved as it is today. Over two thousand years have passed. The worst of the Kali Yuga is over. The Kali Yuga was a time period when our Sun was the farthest from the center of the galaxy. It was a time when the deeper truths of Creation were harder to understand. The time period corresponds roughly to the Dark Ages and the 1000 years leading up to it. In the present, people are able to understand the concepts of Mind, Creation, and the energy and substance that lies beyond the perception of the five physical senses.

Now is the time in humanity's evolution for many to become enlightened. It is also the time for many teachers to come forward. Instead of just one en-LIGHT-ened being to lead an entire race, people or country forward, now is the time for many people to teach and lead the world.

Teach and lead with honesty, truth, love, and LIGHT and there is no need for guile or intellectualism. Such a one can aid the country, the people and the world to prosperity and fulfillment. Intellectualism is brain thinking. Now is the time for more people to do mind thinking. Over and over Lao Tzu counsels us to build wisdom and enlightenment and to not be so concerned with intellectual information or being smart.

The great master Confucius who was a contemporary of Lao Tzu focused his mind on attaining wisdom instead of settling for information accumulation.

In Chapter IV of Book II of the Analects of Confucius,

Confucius – which means the master Chung – says, *"The Master said: 'At fifteen I set my mind upon wisdom. At thirty I stood firm. At forty I was free from doubts. At fifty I understood the laws of Heaven. At sixty my ear was docile. At seventy I could follow the desires of my heart without transgressing the right'."*

There are two alternatives. You can operate, live, reason, and experience as a soul inhabiting a physical body using each experience to learn and grow and progress in soul awareness, or you can be engrossed in the physical body, believe physical life is all there is to creation, be separate and alone, and in the end die in sadness.

The hidden power is in the understanding of the Perfect, Divine Plan of Creation held in Superconscious Mind and living according to that plan and process.

The hidden power is in the seed idea or plan for creation held in Superconscious Mind. It permeates all of Mind including Subconscious and Conscious Mind. Fulfillment comes from living the plan, the seed idea for creation.

Living in accordance, alignment, and attunement to Superconscious Mind leads one to mastery of mind which leads to en-LIGHT-enment. The one who masters mind comes to identify more and more with the unity of Self called I AM, for I AM exists in reality beyond and above Mind, beyond and above time, and space or distance.

In this there is eternal connectedness in LIGHT, love, truth and goodness, in Self, with all beings and all creation.

The lesson is:

Physical knowledge and knowledge from the five senses and brain is limited to temporary physical knowledge only. The knowledge the Mind can provide is unlimited and eternal. Thus to learn to use the mind is essential to knowing Self and creation.

Sixty-six

Why is the sea King of a hundred rivers
because it naturally lies below them
Thus, it is the King of a hundred rivers
Thus, the one who would be above the people
must speak as if he were below them
If he chooses to lead the people
he must walk as if he is behind them
Thus, although the Sage is above
the people are not burdened
When he is in front
the people are not restricted

Therefore,
The world is glad to support his forward movement
Because he does not compete
no one competes against him

The force of gravity causes water to flow downhill. Water flows down the hills to the ditches, from the ditches it flows to the streams, and then to the small rivers, from the small rivers to the large rivers and from the rivers to the ocean or sea. When the water has reached the sea or ocean we say it has reached sea level.

The oceans have more water than all the ditches, streams, and rivers. Yet the ocean constantly receives more water from them. Where does the water from the hills, ditches, streams, and rivers come from? It comes from the oceans. Water evaporates off the oceans, and forms clouds that then are carried by wind to land areas. The clouds then deposit their moisture or water on the land in the form of rain.

Thus there is a continuous cycle of giving and receiving between the land and the ocean, the ocean and the land.

The ocean continuously receives the benefits of the earth and rivers via gravity.

Therefore, one who can receive from everywhere at all times is capable of leading and governing.

To serve with humility to be lower, is to be able, capable, and willing to receive at all times. To serve with humility one must be willing to listen for listening is a form of receptivity. One who listens can learn what others have experienced. Therefore, such a one can make more educated and wise decisions based on more accurate and all inclusive information.

A leader cannot do everything for all the people. They must learn to be responsible and do things for themselves. They must learn to cause success. A Sage, who is a leader must teach teachers and leaders. In this way, the wise one can seem or appear to follow behind physically when in truth he is leading mentally.

How can the people feel oppressed when the leader is receptive and also follows? The receptive leader is able to receive and give love and compassion to and from followers. The en-LIGHT-ened being does no harm rather he is productive. The hallmark of a mental adult is that he always adds to his environment, improving it, prospering it and making it better than he found it.

The mental adult, the Sage, the en-LIGHT-ened being, always adds to everyone and everything and leaves things better than he found them.

Therefore, the whole world which symbolizes all of Mind supports such a one for the urge of creation is forward motion and the building of the LIGHT of creation. And LIGHT is awareness. No one ever tires of fulfillment. Most everyone wants to help someone who has helped them first.

The one who is secure in the Real Self knows I AM and lives life fully in the now, the eternal present. The present is the only time or place that learning, growth and soul evolution can occur. Therefore, each step, each action, each movement is for the progression of Self to enlightenment and attunement to the Creator. When one gives freely, one then receives freely from the bounty of the Universe. Giving and receiving replace struggle and competition for survival.

Therefore, such a one enjoys the freedom of creation which is responsibility. Such a one aids in the upliftment of the consciousness of humanity.

The lesson is:

Learn to receive.
Practice consistent giving and sharing.
Help others to be
successful.

Sixty-seven

The world calls me great
great yet different from everyone else
Yet, it is because I am different from others
that I am able to be great
If I were like everyone else I would
have stayed small and seemed insignificant

I have always had three treasures
that I uphold and keep
The first is compassion
The second is economy
The third is the humility of choosing not to be
ahead of others

One who is compassionate can be courageous
One who is economical can be generous
One who is humble can be the leader
of those who succeed

One who has courage but no compassion
generosity but no economy
leadership but no humility
Is surely doomed

In war compassion brings victory
and is a permanent, lasting defense
When heaven wants to save someone
it protects them with compassion

Most of the world's people lead physical lives because they think physical thoughts. A mental thinker, a spiritual being, does not lead the life for physical reasons. Such a one creates the life for the purpose of adding to the soul and Subconscious Mind which is mental and spiritual reasoning. Such a one, a mental being or thinker, is different from physically thinking people.

Compassion allows one to be good, kind and loving to others and to understand the inherent value of oneself. True treasures are eternal and permanent. They add wholeness and completeness to the soul. They permit and enhance the ability of one to add permanent understandings of creation to the subconscious mind of the individual.

The second treasure of Lao Tzu, economy, provides one the opportunity to make full use of the energy, matter and learning available in one's life. For in economy nothing is wasted and everything is used to the fullest and recycled.

The third treasure is in being willing to be receptive instead of all the time aggressive. It is in the ability to surrender the conscious ego. To be a good leader one must first be a good follower. Lao Tzu embodies and understands both the follower and the leader, the student and the teacher.

To be courageous is to act and be committed even when there is fear. Without fear there is no need for courage. Fears should never be allowed to control or impede the progress of the Self. Often this requires courage.

To be generous requires love, openness, connectedness and intelligence. The one who uses all energy to the fullest is able to recycle energy into Mind for further use in a higher form. Such a one always has enough and always has extra.

Without economy one never has enough and so is afraid to give for fear of losing what is possessed. Therefore, generosity and economy promote compassion.

Without humility the conscious ego controls the Self leading one to folly and greater entrapment in physical matter. When this happens the learning ceases and death ensues. Without learning there is no need for a soul to reside in a physical body. Without a soul, the physical body ceases to exist. This is why without compassion, economy and humility, one begins to die.

Compassion brings victory in war because people cooperate with each other when kindness and love are present. Therefore, no new wars are created. When the victor is mean to the vanquished then the one who loses the war seeks revenge.

The more minds that work together in a common ideal of creation, the more power and strength exist. Interconnectedness of minds to other minds and all of creation is how Superconscious Mind causes there to be eternal life, motion, and learning of the Principles of Creation.

That which is eternal is never destroyed but continually creates and raises the consciousness of the planet and all of creation.

Heaven rejoices as interconnectedness is built in one or many. Heaven is fulfilled as interconnectedness leads to unity consciousness. Compassion and love make greater connectedness possible. Compassion unites.

Humility creates a state of mind where one is always willing to receive and always willing to learn. The good leader is always willing to learn.

One who chooses to place the Real Self above the temporary physical body is different. Most people live their lives based on the accumulation of physical possessions. The Sage, the one who is gaining enlightenment places the fulfillment of Karma and the building of permanent soul understandings as the top priority. Yet permanent understandings of Self and creation are not visible or perceivable by the five senses. The fulfillment of Karma is not visible to the five senses.

Most people choose experiences and place value upon physical, sensory experiences. Yet it is the very factor of permanent understanding that makes one great.

The lesson is:

Continually upgrade the ability to practice compassion, economy, and humbleness in Self and thus become great.

Sixty-eight

Thus, the excellent officer is not violent
the excellent warrior is not angry
the excellent conqueror does not initiate
the excellent commander is humble
This is called the virtue of not competing
this is called using the strength of others
this is called uniting with Heaven
Which since ancient times has been the ideal

68

Lao Tzu says compassion brings victory and is a permanent lasting defense. The excellent offer is not violent and the excellent warrior is not angry because compassion is more powerful. Compassion brings victory.

The excellent conqueror overcomes without battle because compassion is more powerful. The excellent commander is humble because one can be a leader by choosing not to be ahead of others physically while holding a strong, creative image of what is needed to be accomplished. To be humble is to use and direct one's mind instead of being engrossed in the brain and five senses.

When one does not compete with others, the mind is freed and can be directed by the Self to fulfill the individual's destiny instead of trying to fulfill someone else's destiny. To compete with others draws the mind outward. To know the Self, the mind must be directed inward.

Seeing others achieve greatness can cause another person's imagination to be stimulated which then propels one to greater things. This is using the strength of others.

In order to unite with Heaven one must first image the Self as becoming and being enlightened. It is truth that as you think, so you become. Therefore, a thinker will constantly upgrade the thinking ability by imagining the Self as more enlightened and by understanding the Self as the cause of one's life.

The only reason to be armed is because one lives in fear or feels out of control. Anger proceeds from thinking one is not in control. To unite with Heaven is to fulfill the plan in Superconscious Mind and to become fully awake to Self as a creator. To become enlightened has always been the ideal. To know all of Mind and to know Self is the destiny and evolutionary potential of each individual.

The lesson is:
All control and power come from thought and thought beings with the thinker – the individual. Therefore, direct the thoughts of Self productively.

Sixty-nine

In the strategy of warfare there is a saying
Rather than being the host
it is better to be the guest
Rather than advancing an inch
it is better to retreat a foot

This is called
marching without moving
seizing without weapons
engaging without attacking
repulsing without hostility

There is no greater misfortune
than thinking you have an enemy
to think you have an enemy is to be
disconnected from one's greatest treasure

Thus, when opposing forces meet
the one with compassion will surely prevail

To be a host is to receive people into one's house. To receive people is to be receptive.

To be a guest is to travel to see someone in their house. To visit someone is to be aggressive. To act on one's thoughts and desires is to be aggressive. The essence of the teaching is; it is better to be receptive than aggressive.

To advance an inch is to be aggressive which is to initiate activity. To retreat a foot is to leave a space for the other army. This is a type of receptivity. So again the lesson presented is that receptivity is more powerful than the aggressive quality.

This chapter continues the theme or subject of war and peace.

The soldier's job is to break things and kill people. To kill someone is to destroy or remove their learning opportunity for soul growth and spiritual development. To break things is to render them useless.

Therefore, the wise person always seeks to create rather than to destroy, to receive and learn rather than to destroy or avoid the learning opportunity.

The guest moves forward to the host. The host receives the guest.

Rather than risk destroying opportunities for learning, be receptive, stop pushing outward and instead receive inward. This is called marching without moving because the receptive one who is willing to receive the learning always gains and profits. The one who rushes forward aggressively may achieve a physical goal yet fail to receive the soul growth and spiritual development available in the lessons and learning from the experience.

In order to seize the enemy without weapons one must receive. One must be receptive to the situation at hand and either harmonize with it or cause the situation to harmonize with the Self. This is accomplished by giving and receiving love first and by exchanging truth.

Engaging without attacking can be accomplished when love is present. Love is very engaging yet it does not destroy.

Repulsing without hostility occurs when the hostile one learns there are more productive ways to accomplish than using force.

To think you have an enemy is to view the Self as separate from the universe and all other beings. This is not the true reality. The true reality is universal connectedness. Universal connectedness leading to the full awareness and realization of the full oneness of all creation is the greatest treasure. It is Heaven on Earth.

Thus when opposing forces meet, the one without an enemy will surely prevail because the true nature of reality is connectedness. The one who functions from the connectedness of compassion will have the most power.

The lesson is:

Receive the greater truth of connectedness into the Self and gain the power of receptivity. Instead of imagining fears imagine the results desired. Focus on what you desire to create instead of what you do not want to occur.

Seventy

My words are easy to understand
and easy to practice
Yet few are able to understand them
My words come from an ancient source
my actions have a higher master
Because people have no understanding of my words
people do not understand me
those who understand me are few
they who follow my teaching I treasure

Therefore, even if the Sage wears coarse clothing
he holds the jewel of Jade in his heart

70

The Mind is simple. The Mind is simple in that it is uncompli-
cated. The physical, worldly life of sensory engrossment which
entraps the soul in a physical body for a lifetime seems complicated. It appears to be complicated because the five senses create the illusion that everyone and everything is separate.

The truth is everyone and everything is connected. This
connectedness is discerned by the mind. How does one use the
mind to go beyond the illusion of separateness created by the five
senses? Self must still the mind. First concentration is applied to
focus on a single point or object with the full attention. This
focused attention is then applied in meditation to align the Conscious and Subconscious Minds and attune them to the
Superconscious Mind.

The more one stills and quiets the thoughts of the conscious mind, the more one can perceive with the whole mind. A
scattered, distracted, or busy conscious mind with its rapid, attendant thoughts covers up the subconscious and conscious minds
to the engrossed and entrapped soul.

To understand and perform Lao Tzu's words one must quiet
the thoughts and still the mind.

A statement such as, "*Whatever you wish men to do for you,
do likewise also for them; for this is the law and the prophets*" *(Matthew
7:12)* is easy to say, is easy to understand, and seems easy to practice. Yet it requires a disciplined mind and years of practice and
study to learn how to integrate this Universal Truth into one's
consciousness.

Who is willing to practice a 15 or 20 minute concentration
exercise every day? Who is willing to practice 30 or 60 minutes
of meditation every day? How many people are willing to consistently, every day aid others to know themselves? Yet it is pre-
cisely this kind of discipline and service that are necessary to understand the Tao Te Ching and the Universal Truth it contains.

243

The words of the Tao Te Ching describe the workings of the Superconscious Mind. This is the ancient source referred to in this chapter. The actions of an enlightened being are in tune to Superconscious Mind. Superconscious Mind is the higher master.

To understand the words of Lao Tzu one must know the inner Self and the higher divisions of Mind. Few people are willing to discipline the Self, surrender their conscious ego, and go beyond all limitations to know I AM, which is the goal of the Real Self. To follow the teachings of the Sage is to gain a great treasure of permanent or soul learning.

Clothing represents one's outer expression. The outer expression is the way we present ourselves in the physical world. It is the way we appear to others. What is most important is who we really are on the inside. People sometimes put up false fronts, or false presentations. Coarse clothing shows no pretensions. The jewel in the heart symbolizes one filled with love, understanding, and compassion. This is what is most important.

The one who is mentally disciplined and has thus gained the ability to still the mind is able to cause the actions to follow in the same manner. Thus, the actions, activity, and effort are disciplined as is the mind.

The person with an undisciplined mind thinks of everything and everyone as separate and isolated. Such a person cannot understand the one who does everything from a knowing of connectedness. Connectedness promotes creation. Separation brings about destruction. In destruction, the being fails to learn creation.

Most people fail to understand Self as a mental creator. They have yet to understand that thought is cause. They have yet to understand and be fully aware of the thoughts of Self because they have yet to still the mind. Where your attention is, there also is your learning.

Therefore, the knower, the one gaining enlightenment refuses to be engrossed in physical life. Instead, such a one uses physical experiences for the express purpose of soul growth and spiritual development. *"For where your treasure is, there also will be your heart," (Matthew 6:21).*

Permanent understanding of Self and creation is the jewel in the heart. For understandings are an eternal adding to the Self of LIGHT, love, and truth. With these one can create anything and be connected to everything in unity consciousness. The jewel of the heart is the most precious of all riches and wealth in the universe and beyond.

The lesson is:

**Listen
to your inner source, the inner voice,
the voice in the silence
and share your goodness with others.
Know the love and understanding centered
in the Heart.**

Seventy-one

To realize you do not understand
is awareness
To think you understand when you do not
is limitation
The reason the Sage is not limited
is because he recognizes limitations as limitations
Thus he is not limited

The person who thinks, "I know it all," is unwilling to receive new learning.

The one who is willing to learn gains strength and grows in wisdom and understanding.

The one who realizes, "I have a lot to learn," is willing and capable of learning.

When you stop learning you begin to die. In that death is the removal of attention from physical existence. The purpose of physical existence is to learn.

Knowing one's weaknesses one is able to concentrate on improving in those areas until weakness becomes strength. One who knows the limitations of Self has the opportunity to expand beyond those limitations.

Refusing to gain knowledge is the refusal to receive. People starve when they refuse to receive food. The soul starves when the Self in the conscious mind refuses to pursue new learning and new understanding. Knowledge of creation built into permanent understandings of creation is nourishment or food for the soul.

Pain is brought about by thoughts and attitudes that are unproductive. Pain brings our attention to something we need to change.

The one who realizes there is yet a lot to learn has awareness. Desiring the greatest learning, which is knowledge of Self, shows or indicates awareness.

To think "I understand" when this is not so, keeps a person from making the effort to learn more.

To recognize all stages of being as a reference point for greater learning and growth in consciousness, gives one the opportunity to continuously learn and build permanent knowledge of all of Mind and Self.

This continual ability to learn and progress in all situations at all times overcomes any and all limitations in consciousness. If there is no recognition of limitation where is the motivation to go beyond the limitation? Reasoning beings who are in touch with the inner Self realize they have limitations and need to expand the awareness and consciousness to go beyond these limitations.

This motivation to overcome all obstacles, which are really limitations in consciousness, is what produces an enlightened being – a Sage.

The lesson is:

***Always be willing to learn.
Have an open mind. Realize there is much to learn.***

Seventy-two

When the people no longer fear authority
a greater authority is about to manifest
do not restrict people in their own houses
do not suppress them as they earn their livelihood
If they are not suppressed
They won't protest

Thus, the Sage knows the Self
but does not display himself boastfully
has love and compassion
but does not exalt himself
Therefore, he releases the latter which is the outer
and chooses the former which is the inner

When people go beyond the darkness or lack of awareness which is fear, they function from love and truth.

When people no longer fear authority, the higher or greater authority is about to manifest. This higher authority is the inner Self, the soul, the subconscious mind, the spirit or I AM. Fear keeps one locked in the brain. The higher authority is known through the use of the mind.

Thus, restriction will never bring about greater learning or growth in awareness. People protest against restriction when what they really need to learn is responsibility – the ability to respond.

Therefore, listen to the inner authority and create the life that the inner Self designed.

The Sage does not accept restriction because there is constant movement to go beyond limitations. The Sage has greater authority because he has gone beyond limitations in consciousness. The Sage has Self value which comes from knowing what is lasting, permanent, and eternal. The reasoner focuses all the attention on building up the whole Self in ways that will last forever.

The one who is secure in the Self never has to prove this to others. The one who knows the Self is always real. Therefore, the one with eyes to see can perceive the enlightened one. The Self value of such a one is obvious and does not need to be demonstrated.

An enlightened being chooses to remain focused on the Real Self, the inner Self, the lasting and eternal Self. Meanwhile, the temporary forms and limitations of physical life are released and replaced by the everlasting light of awareness. The Sage chooses the inner because it is lasting and permanent. The outer or physical life is temporary. The value of physical life is in building permanent understandings of Self and creation.

Thus, physical life has great value. Yet most people fail to discern and use its true value. Instead, they opt for sensory experience alone.

Symbolically, a house represents one's mind. This is true whether the house appears in a dream or in a Holy Book. The statement *"do not restrict people in their own houses"* is a command or petition for each individual to examine limitations in consciousness, for limited thinking produces restriction in the ability to produce success in one's life – be it mental, emotional, or physical.

All successful people do certain things with their minds that unsuccessful people do not. The biggest difference is successful people do not accept limitations in their thoughts. Therefore, these people go beyond limitations in their life. Limitations or restrictions can be mental, emotional or physical. The successful person, the superior person goes beyond all three. Self discipline is employed to achieve the greatest dreams and aspirations.

When one uses discipline of Self daily to excel then one does not feel suppressed and, therefore, one does not need to blame or protest against another. All success begins with Self value which is the belief in the Self and one's capabilities to achieve.

It is a question of whether the individual chooses to use the time of a life to experience temporariness or whether the time and effort is invested in building the permanent and lasting.

The lesson is:

Act on goals, ideals, needs, the greatest desires and dreams that one holds most dear. Accept no limitations in Self. Believe in Self and the power of the mind.

Seventy-three

Brave in being daring leads to death
bravery without daring preserves life
of these two
one benefits the other harms
Some things Heaven is against
who knows the reason
The Way of Heaven does not strive
yet is good at overcoming
The Way of Heaven does not speak
yet is good at answering
is not summoned yet comes on its own
is patient yet follows a plan
Heaven's net is all encompassing
though its meshes are wide nothing slips through

The Divine Plan is that each I AM, each soul, each person should become a creator, fully enlightened. Each I AM is eternal. Each person's duty is to come to realize, know and understand the eternal nature of Self. Each person's duty is to come to know Self as LIGHT, love and truth. The great plan of creation, the Tao, will be and is being fulfilled. It wins because it is eternally giving.

The Divine Plan has all the time in the world. In fact, all the time in the Universe because the Divine or Perfect Plan is above or beyond space and time.

Space is distance and distance is how physical time is measured.

This Divine Plan is constantly drawing us and urging the soul to fulfill its mission of soul growth and spiritual development which is the movement to en-LIGHT-enment.

The Divine Plan of Creation is whole and complete. Its vehicle for manifestation is LIGHT. Mind is LIGHT taking on form. Mind is the vehicle I AM uses to learn to know Self and how to be a creator.

Being whole the Divine Plan is complete. The thinker fulfills the Divine Plan within the Self by the action and motion of creation, by learning creation, and by understanding how to cause creation.

The Divine Plan of Creation is in every atom and every molecule of creation. In deep meditation, Heaven or Superconscious Mind always answers and comes because the meditation becomes connected to all.

The Divine Plan is in gases, minerals, plants, animals, humans, and spiritual beings. It is in all things. It permeates the universe for the universe is interconnected and no-thing is separate.

A brave and passionate or daring person will fight for certain beliefs or ideas.

A brave and calm person will create and preserve peace.

A brave and calm person has the courage and fortitude to discipline the mind so as to bring it to obey the Self.

A still and quiet mind experiences peace. Therefore, there is no warring either within Self or with others. Warring with others begins by warring within Self.

Peace on Earth occurs when every person experiences and creates peace in Self. Peace benefits. Fighting harms. A still, peaceful mind can create.

A busy, fighting mind destroys.

A still mind is a receptive mind.

A fighting mind is constantly creating mental pictures or images.

The Way of Heaven does not strive yet is good at overcoming because Heaven or Superconscious Mind continuously is at peace and freely gives. To create and add to what is already present is good and true for it is eternal. To destroy or take away from Self or what is in the environment is harmful for it prevents or delays lastingness from being built within the Self or others.

Heaven, which is the Superconscious Mind, favors creation over destruction because the Divine or Perfect Plan of Creation is held within Superconscious Mind. Heaven or Superconscious Mind favors eternal creation for this is the Divine Plan created by the Creator. The Creator continuously gives. The Creator gives unconditional love continuously.

Heaven or Superconscious Mind favors eternal creation for this is the Divine Plan created by the Creator. All are continually provided with the inner urge to become whole, to know the Self, and to mature as a mental and spiritual being.

Individuals, having the ability to choose, have the choice of either living in greater oneness of connectedness of love or of avoiding the truth of connectedness. Avoiding the truth leads to existence in the false perception of separation.

The Divine Plan of Creation, referred to as *"the Way of Heaven"* in this chapter, is in Superconscious Mind. It reaches all, touches all, and is at the essence of all. Therefore, sooner or later it brings all beings to a higher, more expanded level of consciousness in accordance with the Creator's will.

The lesson is:

Develop and practice courage with a still mind.
Use this courage to create and go beyond limitations.
Give freely and receive abundantly.

Seventy-four

If people no longer fear death
what is the purpose of threatening to kill them
But suppose the people did fear death
and still acted in perverse and devious ways
and we caught and convicted them
who would dare to kill them
As long as people fear death
there will always be an executioner
To kill in place of the executioner
is like cutting wood in place of the master
carpenter
Those that try to take the place of the master
carpenter
will almost always hurt their own hands

Death, interpreted using the Universal Language of Mind, symbolizes change. What is considered to be physical death of a person is actually the movement of attention or consciousness of the soul away from the conscious mind and physical body, permanently. In order for people to fear death, they must have some pleasure or benefit from physical life. Life is an opportunity for learning and growth. Withdrawal of the soul's attention from the physical body means that the opportunity for soul learning is over or gone.

Self is a soul. The Self is not a physical body. The soul is I AM in Subconscious Mind. When a person learns to cause productive change, which is adding to one's consciousness, then there is less fear of external change in the environment.

The nature of physical life is change. Nature goes through the changing of the seasons. The universe operates in cycles.

Death symbolizes change. The function of death is a movement in consciousness. Each person needs to move consciousness forward – every day.

The consciousness of each individual needs to expand continuously.

The more one causes productive, consistent changes, the less one fears change.

The best change is always accompanied by growth.

Change is good.

Never destroy another person's opportunities for learning. Always use opportunities to learn. A person who lives in fear will tend to live by rules instead of reasoning. A person who lives in fear has the reasoning capabilities impaired.

Sometimes physical rules do not correspond to mental laws, spiritual laws, and Universal Laws.

Since Universal Laws are omnipresent, one who thinks, feels, or acts in ways that are not in harmony with the Universal Laws experiences pain and sorrow.

The executioner symbolizes the one who is able to cause change. To fear death symbolizes a fear of change. The one who tries to cause change by destroying only ends up destroying the learning opportunities for the Self. This produces isolation, disassociation, separation and disconnectedness.

A hand symbolizes purpose when interpreted in the Universal Language of Mind. One who attempts to change physical life without purpose ends up destroying.

One cannot pretend to be a creator, an enlightened being. Instead cause Self to learn to create every day.

Only through giving will one receive.

Only through complete giving will one receive completely.

Master change.

Experience ful-fill-ment.

One cannot live in fear and be an enlightened being.

One cannot live in fear and be a conscious, enlightened creator.

Fear destroys when dwelled upon and practiced.

Live in harmony with Universal Law and gain purpose.

Have the courage to change.

Have the courage to grow.

The lesson is:
Make choices every day, that require one to think and reason. Make choices that are not habits or one's usual way of thinking and being. Thus overcome habits.

Seventy-five

Why are the people hungry and starving
it is a result of over taxation by the rulers
That is why the people are hungry and starving

Why are the people rebellious and hard to rule
it is because those above them interfere too much
     in their lives
That is why the people are rebellious and hard to rule

What is the reason the people think so little of death
it is because the rulers demand too much of their life
that is why the people think little of death
Meanwhile those who do nothing to produce life
seem to be esteemed above those who love life

Lao Tzu was a conservative in that he advocated smaller and less intrusive government. He taught that people should have the freedom to learn and succeed.

Consider a nation as having many people and people symbolizing the aspects of Self. Then is it seen that a smaller government and lower taxes represent one who values the ability to make choices and be responsible for those choices. Taxation by the government takes the money from the people who earn the money and gives it to other people to administer. This is highly inefficient. Lao Tzu praised economy. Inefficiency is not economy. A still mind is a very efficient mind.

The thought in the Tao Te Ching is that people should be able to live their lives without much outside interference.

Why are children without both parents most of the day and many times at night? The answer is because taxes are too high. Taxes are so high that both Mother and Father have to work at an outside job. Therefore, a babysitter or day care center, or the government in the form of pre-schools and kindergarten (kid-garden), is raising their children.

Government raising the children destroys the next generation's choice making ability and imagination. When imagination is destroyed the productivity of the children and society and a country is destroyed.

The people are starving because government takes their money from them. It promised them protection and that it will take care of them, but in the end people are slaves, living in fear and destitution. Therefore, people rebel. They want change. They want the freedom to grow.

People want opportunities to be responsible. They want the freedom to learn and grow and be successful. Therefore, look to perceive the ways in which one wastes time, energy, and money every day and eliminate waste.

People are starving for soul growth and spiritual development. They want the truth. They want the truth of creation and LIGHT and of their existence.

People rebel against limitations. Each person needs a place to create in order to expand the consciousness beyond limitation.

The nature of Subconscious Mind is forward motion.

The nature of consciousness is expansion.

When people are taught to be productive, and to be responsible, and to create and given the opportunity to do so there is no need to rebel.

An adult always adds to what exists within the environment. A reasoner, a mental adult, improves upon what exists in the environment.

When one's attention is fully fixed on survival there is little time or energy for soul growth. Therefore, people want the time and energy for soul growth and en-LIGHT-enment. When people are engrossed in their day-to-day physical lives they do not think of death because it is in the future.

The more one uses each day for quickening one's soul growth and spiritual development, the more one treasures each day as an opportunity for further illumination of Self.

Therefore, give attention to the inner, Divine Self every day.

Love life and love others whether or not you gain esteem from it. Life is motion. Produce greater forward motion in the life.

The lesson is:

Use everything to the fullest. Do not waste opportunities. Instead love life.

Seventy-six

When people are born
they are supple and soft
when they die
they are rigid and stiff
When plants grow rapidly
they are soft and tender
when they die
they are withered and dry

Therefore, it is said
the unyielding and rigid are followers of death
the soft and yielding are followers of life
when an army becomes rigid it suffers defeat
when a plant becomes hard it ends
Thus, the hard and rigid are from below
the soft and yielding are from above

Supple and soft symbolize the ability to change, to adjust, and adapt. Hard and stiff indicates one who is incapable or has difficulty changing, adjusting, and adapting. Infancy is a time of rapid learning. Infancy is the time of most rapid learning for the child absorbs knowledge and learning like a sponge absorbs water.

Water is an excellent example for flexibility. Water is fluid. It can change shape depending upon the vessel it is poured into.

People tend to slow down in their learning the older they get. Therefore, it is very important that each individual accept a program of Self discipline in order to learn how to keep the mind open to learning. When the mind is open, there is no end to the learning. To become enlightened, one must be willing to constantly learn, to transform old worn-out ideas by accepting a greater truth. The true security is not in what one learned years ago, but in how one is applying what one learned years ago to gain greater learning today. The present, the eternal now, is the only time to grow in consciousness.

The physical body is mostly water. At birth, there is a lot of water in the body. Most people become dehydrated as they age. As they get older they get more dry and brittle just like plants. Water is a symbol for the experiences of the conscious mind in the physical life. The nature of life is motion. The nature of the physical universe is change. Therefore, it is important that one moves forward in life, adapting, adjusting and adding to one's consciousness in order to use the life experiences wisely.

The more one is willing to change, grow and adapt, the more one remains flexible enough to respond to the inner urge to know creation and the inner and outer changes of life.

The sap of tender, green plants contains an abundance of life force and water. As a person begins to die the life force begins to withdraw from the physical body. Life is receptive. One who is filled with life is open, eager, and receptive to new experiences and new learning.

A stiff and unbending person is one who refuses to receive new learning in the conscious life experiences but instead tries to make new learning fit into old, outworn, smallish concepts of physical existence.

The more people refuse to learn the smaller their world gets until finally their world shrinks down to a size smaller than their physical body. At this point they die which is in effect, the soul choosing to withdraw attention from the physical body. The soul places attention in Subconscious Mind once again. Without a soul to animate it, the physical body dies. At death there is no longer the intelligent direction of the soul holding the organs, cells, molecules, and atoms of the physical body together. Thus, the body deteriorates.

The receptive one, the learning one continues to live. The one who gets fixed in the old ways dies. When plants or people grow rapidly they are soft and tender. To learn and grow is a choice that any of us can make at any time. Choose life. Learn to release limited and false concepts of life, of others, and of the Self.

The urge of consciousness is expansion.

A mind that is growing, learning, and receiving expands.

A mind that is closed off contracts.

Too much contraction leads to restriction which is ultimately death.

The mind that is hard and closed off cannot learn that is why they are followers of death.

LIGHT is not limited. Consciousness which is a vehicle of LIGHT is not limited until restricted by the thoughts in the conscious mind of one who mentally tries to live in the past. This is why the soft and yielding are followers of life. They live in the present, the eternal now. A child, an infant, lives in the now. They see something and they want it now. A thought or idea that manifests into physical form immediately crystallizes and begins becoming more rigid. The thinker slows down the rate that a creation becomes rigid so the manifested thought structure can last and be used longer.

The past is over. The Self has the opportunity to grow and expand in the present. An army that is rigid cannot change. Therefore, when events in the environment or new innovation by the opposing army ensues, the rigid lose because they cannot adjust or adapt.

The one who learns, grows, changes, and receives is able to adapt in changing conditions. The hard and strong are from below because below indicates physical entrapment. The soft and yielding are from above because above indicates Heaven or Superconscious Mind.

Humbleness is the willingness to be open to receive. Humbleness aids one to be soft and yielding. The more humble one is the more capable one is of receiving.

One who is closed off to receiving can never give.

A baby receives everything and gives love. A baby is soft. Eternal life is like a baby.

The lesson is:

**Be soft and yielding,
which is to have an open mind, to recieve
new ideas and to live and grow in the eternal
now.**

Seventy-seven

The Way of Heaven
is like stringing a bow
the high is pulled down
and the low is raised up
Where there is too much it diminishes
Where there is not enough it adds to

The Way of Heaven
takes from the excess
and gives to the lacking
unlike the way of man
which is to take from those in need
and give to those who have too much
Who is the one who can have more than is needed
and give it to the world
Only those who live by the Way

Therefore, the Sage initiates activity
without being possessed by it
accomplishes tasks without attachments
illumines without displaying his greatness

The goal of each person is to cause Heaven on Earth.

This is the goal that is needed, for mankind is to cause Heaven on Earth.

Raise the consciousness of Self up to Heaven which is Superconscious Mind.

Bring the awareness of Superconscious Mind or Heaven into the waking conscious mind.

Bring Heaven which is Superconscious awareness into all that is said, thought, and done.

"The high is pulled down" means to bring superconscious awareness into one's waking awareness.

"The low is raised up" means to lift one's consciousness up to Superconscious Mind.

Let all interactions be between two or more beings of LIGHT. In fact, let there be no between, for between indicates separation.

Instead let there by universal connectedness in which distance, or the separation and isolation of the Self, is obliterated.

The ideal of Self is to master distance and separation and thereby live in continual connectedness and the eternal present. In this way master space and time.

Maintain and add to the expanded consciousness of Self every day.

Be willing to adjust the string of your consciousness in all that you do.

When something is not working, when one's efforts are not producing success, or when life is not fulfilling, then change. The Way of Heaven diminishes when there is too much because nature and all of Mind seek a balance and harmony.

Where there is not enough, the Way of Heaven adds to,

for the same reason. When one changes, then one's life changes and the world changes. Therefore, there is once again room for growth and learning.

Those who aid others to abundance in turn receive greater abundance. This is the Universal Law of Abundance.

Since the Superconscious Mind or Heaven contains the balance of the Aggressive and Receptive Principles of Creation, its nature is to take from the excess and give to the lacking. This produces balance.

Creation proceeds from balance to imbalance to balance once again. Nature seeks balance. Consciousness creates imbalance in order to receive the learning from forward motion.

Greed causes one to become poor, for greed stops the learning process.

Greed makes it difficult for one to receive.

When people share, the total wealth is increased. When people share, there is fulfillment. Heaven or Superconscious Mind always seeks to balance things. When people share, there is giving and receiving. When there is the free flow of goods and services everyone has the opportunity to succeed. The spiritual being, the one with an abundance of prana or life force and an elevated, expanded consciousness has more than enough. Such a one knows how to receive and therefore gives freely.

The person of the Tao is the enlightened thinker who has learned to tap a never ending supply of life force from Superconscious Mind which is Heaven.

The Sage is motivated from the inner soul urge to expand the consciousness into Universal connectedness and unity consciousness which is union with the Godhead which is the overcoming of limitations and the illusion of space, of distance, and of time. Such a one lives in the eternal now. The consciousness of such a one creates the future from the present. Such a one gives activity, action, and motion without forming emotional attachments. Such a one has a disciplined, surrendered ego and is thus capable of illumining by teaching.

Life is the continual transformation of energy to a higher state of consciousness in order that I AM may know LIGHT as a creator.

The lesson is:

**Cause there to be Heaven on Earth.
Give freely. Live according to needs and
live a disciplined life.**

Seventy-eight

Nothing in this world is softer and weaker than
water
and yet against the hard and strong
nothing is better
for nothing can replace it
The soft overcomes the hard
the weak overcomes the strong
Everyone knows this
yet no one applies and practices it

Therefore, the Sage says
the one who accepts a country's disgrace
we call the lord of Earth and grain
the one who accepts responsibility
for a country's misfortune
we call the king of all under Heaven
These upright words seem upside down

The softness in water makes young plants soft and pliable. Young plants are full of life and water. Softer, weaker, and water are all better against the strong. Therefore, the willingness to be receptive = soft and receive help = weak is much more powerful than thinking one knows it all.

Water is an essential part of all plants and animals on Earth. In this is seen the power of water. Water also symbolizes our conscious, waking, life experiences in the physical world. These life experiences have the power to wear down all our rough edges just as a running stream of water wears off the rough edges of stones so that all is smooth.

The willingness to receive water into the body aids the body to be more flexible and soft. The willingness to receive the learning in our life experiences enables us to be more yielding and flexible in the way we respond and gives us greater ability to respond. So it is important to be willing to adjust, adapt, and to transform one's consciousness constantly just as running water constantly wears down the rough edges of a stone making it smooth and more round.

What can withstand a flooding river or a giant tidal wave? Yet what is more refreshing to drink than water or more refreshing to bathe in?

Running water causes stones at the bottom of a stream to be smooth.

The one who is receptive constantly grows in knowledge and understanding. And knowledge applied is power.

The one who receives, grows. The one who is stiff and unyielding is unable to learn, adapt, and grow and therefore dies.

The en-LIGHT-ened are very receptive. The unenlightened, those still engrossed in physical matter live in the past, in their memories and are therefore unwilling to allow new thoughts into the mind that would override or discredit their old thoughts. Even though the old thoughts are limitations or even wrong.

Everyone knows one must listen in order to learn yet few listen.

To listen is to change.

To receive is to be changed.

Most people are too busy pursuing their engrossed desires to take time to listen, much less to cause the Self to be receptive.

To gain the maximum ability to receive, one must learn to still the mind.

A busy mind is fixed on pursuing a physical desire.

A still and quiet mind pursues the inner Self. The inner Self or soul is always urging the outer conscious mind to learn, grow, and gain in soul growth and spiritual development.

To accept a country's disgrace is to admit a mistake. To accept responsibility for a country's misfortune is to admit making a mistake. To admit making a mistake does not make one great or a ruler, king. To admit making a mistake is the beginning of greatness. It is the beginning of initiating and receiving new learning.

He who is willing to receive the learning from each experience, whether it be pleasurable or painful, comes to master the Self. Such a one comes to master the mind. To admit one made a mistake is not the same as being receptive. Receptivity is much more powerful.

The one who can see the opportunity to consciously create and adds to any situation proves Self to be a creator. Such a one has mastered the lessons of physical life, emotional life, and mental life. Such a one controls and directs all aspects of the life of Self.

This truth makes sense and is easy to understand for Mind

is simple and not complicated. It is the discipline and application of mind into the life and consciousness that most people find difficult or arduous.

Life only seems complicated to those who do not understand Mind.

The Truth only seems to be a paradox for those who neither know Self nor understand Mind.

Just because one admits making a mistake does not make one enlightened nor a great leader. This is why Lao Tzu says, *"These upright words seem upside down."* Admitting you made a mistake is a beginning step in honesty. Honesty promotes truth and truth promotes alignment with Universal Truth.

The lesson is:

Be receptive. Receive the learning.

Seventy-nine

When settling a bitter dispute
some resentment is sure to remain
How could this be regarded as good
Therefore, the Sage keeps his half of the bargain
but does not insist on what he is due from others
Therefore, the person with power
is responsible concerning debts
the person without integrity
requires others to pay their debt
The Tao of Heaven favors no one over the other
yet it always helps the good

Joshua, or Jeshua (Jesus) the Messiah who came to be called the Greek word Christ or Cristos said, *"Try to get reconciled with your accuser promptly, while you are going on the road with him; for your accuser might surrender you to the judge, and the judge would commit you to the jailer, and you would be cast into prison,"* (Matthew 5:25).

Therefore, respond from a point of cause, not effect. Respond before the changes in life overpower the Self.

Instead of having a bitter or angry dispute and then settling it only to have resentment remain, why not do something different? Maintain the correct mental attitude so that disputes do not arise. Try to help others as much as possible. Endeavor to aid others. Be a friend and be kind to others thereby there is no need for disputes. As one does these things for others the same is accomplished within the Self. The one who cares and gives to others finds one's self value increases. As one is kind to others, the capacity within Self to receive from others and the universe increases thereby giving Self a greater fulfillment.

When you have been hurt mentally, emotionally, or physically, the hurt is retained as a memory. That memory leaves in its wake resentment, anger, low self esteem, self pity and most of all fear.

Therefore, do as you say you will do and what you have agreed to do. Have a good, positive, productive, mental attitude. Examine the past in the LIGHT of day with full awareness and not in silence.

The more you live in the past, the more you will live in pain.

The past is over. Change, growth, and illumination can only occur in the present. Therefore, complete everything in the present.

By living fully in the now you can create the possible future. The future of your imaginings.

Revenge is of the past. Revenge keeps you in the past. Therefore, the learned thinker, the smart woman and the intelligent being live fully in the now.

A person who lives the life according to Universal Truth is able to respond to the current situation and thus practices responsibility.

A person who lives a dishonest life, one who thinks one thing and says another, who says one thing and does a different thing or acts contrary to what he has said, has yet to align conscious and subconscious minds. Therefore, such a one is not a responsible being.

The conscious mind self must respond to the inner urge from the inner Self, the soul.

The Perfect and Divine Plan of Creation held in Superconscious Mind is available at all times to those who have lifted their consciousness to receive life force and guidance from the High Self.

Karma may be defined as indebtedness as an individual. Karma is created by intention and relieved by understanding. One must understand the lesson of life in order to relieve karma. To understand the lesson of life is to be permanently transformed in one's total consciousness and being. Through practicing integrity concerning physical debts, one comes to greater awareness of how to relieve mental debts which are the debts owed to the Self. In India, these self-debts are called Karma.

"The person without integrity requires others to uphold their debts," says Chapter 79. This indicates one who thinks physical which is to think of Self as separate from others. Most of the world's ills could be relieved if and when people come to know their connectedness with all other beings. Why cause hardship on another when the other is connected to the Self? This is just being hard on the Self and making learning painful.

277

The enlightened ones are able to accomplish seemingly miraculous activities such as healing because they are able to tap into a higher form of energy and consciousness. This higher source of energy and consciousness is omnipresent and has great power.

The Tao of Heaven always helps the good because all of creation and all of mind is filled with LIGHT. The LIGHT pervades everything unless a person tries to block the LIGHT through hate, or other unproductive thought. The good are always aligned with LIGHT thus LIGHT can help them. LIGHT is always available. Only the good are able to avail themselves of it.

The lesson is:

Always give.

Eighty

Imagine an ideal small state with a small population
where there are labor saving machines
that no one uses
Let the people consider death seriously
and do not think about moving far away
They may have boats and carts
but they have no reason to use them
The people return to the old custom
of the knotting of rope for record keeping
The people enjoy their food
and appreciate their clothing
are content with their homes
find joy in their life
Let the neighboring state be so near
that people hear its dogs and chickens
Yet the people might live out their lives
without traveling back and forth

The topic of this chapter is connectedness and valuing the present moment. When the attention is in the present moment and the present experience then people can grow and learn and be fulfilled. The only place and time that people can learn and grow in consciousness is in the present, the eternal now. This is the reason that in the ideal state described in this chapter people do not travel far away, they do not have weapons and armor or if they do they do not use them. They value and appreciate their food, their homes and customs. To live in the present moment and to value the experience in the present moment is very powerful. It affords the opportunity to receive what is needed into the Self. It is a life of connectedness.

The real life is based on connectedness. The false life is based on separation.

In the country, people wave hello to each other when they meet on the road whether they know each other or not.

In the big cities often they don't wave at each other except in anger. They don't always even look at each other on the street.

The thinker knows life and Mind to be simple because all is interconnected.

Thinking life to be complicated because of separative thinking, the engrossed worldly person needs machines to take the place of the use of Mind.

The closer one is to nature the more one experiences the cycles of change, of birth and death, of the changing of the seasons, of eggs hatching into birds.

The people in big cities and big government are removed from death and also life.

You do not have to protect yourself from your neighbors when you know your neighbors.

In a large city people may not know their neighbors.

Most people do not know themselves. Most people do not know who they are. In connectedness, people can come to know who they are. A person can come to know the Self.

Life is nourishing when people live in friendship. When there is friendship there is connectedness. In connectedness, one can learn and know the true reality.

People can hide in big cities. In small towns everyone knows everyone else. So people often are responsible to each other.

The food is enjoyed and the clothes in Lao Tzu's ideal state are appreciated because the mind is not restless. When the mind is restless it constantly seeks out new sensory stimulation from the environment. Let undivided attention provide the stimulus rather than depending on the environment for this. Create purpose for life, then one always has more than stimulus – one has motivation.

When the mind is still and quiet the Self receives the inner urge and the inner peace which is greater, more pleasing, and more satisfying than sensory stimuli.

People who cause an alignment of their conscious and subconscious minds appreciate the natural sounds of nature more than artificial sounds.

The natural thinker wields the simpleness of mind. This is power.

Since peaceful neighbors live in peace and possess a still, quiet, peaceful mind they are able to live in peace with others.

Living in peace, they live long and prosper. This is because peace is healthy.

The one who begins to cultivate peace within the Self through stilling the mind is able to build this peace in all aspects of the Self. Such a one is then able to maintain peace in all places, at all times, in all situations. The calm mind is disciplined to be under the power and control of the thinker.

It is easy to love when one is peaceful. Cause one's life to be simple as one gains the peace that surpasseth all understanding.

The lesson is:

Be fulfilled, peaceful and content with every minute of every day. Still the mind and savor each experience.

Eighty-one

True words are not beautiful
beautiful words are not true
those who are wise are not smart
those who are smart are not wise
those who are good do not argue
those who argue are not good

The Sage never stores things up
the more he does for others
the more he gains
the more he gives to others
the greater abundance he receives
The Tao of Heaven
is to benefit without harming
The Way of the Sage
is to accomplish with freedom of motion

Truthful words are not beautiful to one who does not want to hear the truth or avoids the truth.

Truthful words are often not easy to receive when they are presented without love, tenderness, kindness and compassion.

Truthful words bring hope to the one who desires rapid soul growth and spiritual development.

The loving teacher is the most beautiful person on earth to the earnest student.

Beautiful words may stir one to emotion. Yet emotions can cloud one's reasoning when suppressed or when they are doing the opposite of suppression which is blowing out.

Since most people do not want to change and accepting greater truth involves changes and the growth of consciousness, most people do not find the truth beautiful.

Just because someone says pretty words that flatter doesn't mean those words are the truth. To be smart as indicated in this chapter is to be able to get what one wants to accomplish physically. To be wise is to know how to teach a person's soul.

Good people do not argue because they seek the truth. All thinkers want to find the truth, receive the truth, practice and apply truth in order to more fully incorporate truth into Self. The purpose of communication is to arrive at a greater truth.

Truth and Love together make LIGHT. LIGHT is split into the Aggressive and Receptive Principles of Creation that are also called Yang and Yin.

In our physical universe and physical environment the Receptive Principle of Creation is mostly seen, felt and experienced as love.

In our physical universe and physical environment the Aggressive Principle of Creation is mostly seen, felt and experienced as truth.

Therefore thinking, reasoning people seek truth enveloped in Love. This eliminates argument.

To argue is to try to force your point of view on another.

Truth given in Love to those desiring to hear and come to know the truth never requires force for the earnest student is eager to receive.

To read a thousand books or see a thousand plays, or hear a thousand lectures does not make one wise.

Many people say, "I know Metaphysics, I have been studying it for 20 years!" While the truth is that these same people have only been reading metaphysical books for 20 years. Reading books is not knowing. It is information, sometimes stored as memory.

Reading a book provides information for the brain. It does not feed the soul. Meditation, dream interpretation, concentration, stilling the mind, mantras or chanting and prana or breathwork provide soul growth and rapid spiritual quickening.

Metaphysical books serve the purpose of stimulating the desire to want to know Universal Truth and Universal Law. And to know how to fully incorporate and integrate that truth into the whole Self one needs a teacher.

Metaphysical books also serve the purpose of providing a framework and vocabulary for teaching others the truth of Mind and Creation.

The wise always causes the energy of Self to flow freely and completely. Therefore, the en-LIGHT-ened one gives and receives freely.

The more one gives, the more one receives. The more one gives to anyone freely without expecting recompense from that one person, the more one is free to receive of the abundance of the universe. It has been said, "Nature abhors a void." Giving creates a space within Self to receive. Nature or the universe loves to fill that space that has been created in the Self through the act of giving.

As one continues giving freely one experiences a greater abundance received from the abundance of the universe.

The Tao of Heaven or Superconscious Mind is to benefit without harming because it goes right to the heart of the individual and rewards those who give freely many times over.

The one with a still mind and single pointed attention created through concentration is free to learn the power of Heaven. The way of the Tao.

The Tao of the Sage is work without effort because the intelligent person, the one who knows the secrets of creation performs all activity with an ideal and purpose in mind. To such a one there is no work there is only learning-filled activity.

The one in whom the energy flows freely with no restrictions knows activity as the full manifestation of one's thoughts from the Subconscious Mind into physical existence. Such a one uses activity or effort as a productive tool to build understandings of Creation and thereby quicken soul growth.

Worldly, physically engrossed and entrapped people pursue the temporary such as sense gratification and accumulation of physical objects. Spiritual and intuitive thinkers and beings pursue the lasting, permanent, and eternal. The Sage has freedom of motion in mind and therefore the freedom to create. Thus, the Sage is able to accomplish much for Self and others.

Permanent understandings of Self and creation are eternal and lasting. LIGHT, Love and Truth are eternal and permanent. Soul growth and spiritual development which is the quickening into LIGHT is eternal.

The lesson is:

***Live the life for the eternal, the lasting,
the permanent and the Real.
Give freely and receive. Seek and you shall find.
Knock and it shall be opened unto you.
Come to know the interconnectedness of all of
Mind and of all Creation.***

Epilogue

There is a Higher Knowledge, a Higher Truth, a Higher Awareness and a Higher Enlightenment that is available to all. It is time for more people to wake up, learn, and be taught this Higher Knowledge.

Before one can learn to use this Higher Knowledge and energy, one has to become aware that it exists. This book serves the purpose of bringing the awareness of the High Knowledge and wisdom to the student.

In order to grow in awareness and consciousness, one must receive knowledge and wisdom that adds to one's consciousness. Therefore it is imperative that each person cultivate the receptive quality.

To improve the ability to receive the Highest Truth, one must learn to still the mind.

There is great power in the still mind.

The still mind is capable of great receptivity and therefore has great drawing power.

The still mind may also initiate productive action which is the use of the Aggressive Principle.

Still the mind. Receive the enlightenment and know the Real Self, the High Self as I AM.

About the Author

Throughout this lifetime, Daniel R. Condron has strived to understand the secrets of life and to explain them in a form that is understandable to all. He first accomplished this as a young boy when he gained a connectedness with nature being in the woods and pastures while growing up on the family farm in northwest Missouri. He has devoted his life to understanding what is permanent and lasting and to knowing the true reality. This he teaches to others. He resides with his wife Barbara and son Hezekiah on the campus of the College of Metaphysics.

Additional titles available from SOM Publishing include:

Atlantis: The History of the World Vol. 1
Drs. Daniel & Barbara Condron ISBN: 0944386-28-8 $15.00

How to Raise an Indigo Child
Dr. Barbara Condron ISBN: 0944386-29-6 $14.00

Interpreting Dreams for Self Discovery
Dr. Laurel Clark & Paul Blosser ISBN: 0944386-25-3 $12.00

Karmic Healing
Dr. Laurel Clark ISBN: 0944386-26-1 $15.00

The Bible Interpreted in Dream Symbols
Drs. Condron, Condron, Matthes, Rothermel
ISBN: 0944386-23-7 $18.00

Spiritual Renaissance
Elevating Your Conciousness for the Common Good
Dr. Barbara Condron ISBN: 0944386-22-9 $15.00

Superconscious Meditation
Kundalini & the Understanding of the Whole Mind
Dr. Daniel R. Condron ISBN 0944386-21-0 $13.00

First Opinion: Wholistic Health Care in the 21st Century
Dr. Barbara Condron ISBN 0944386-18-0 $15.00

The Dreamer's Dictionary
Dr. Barbara Condron ISBN 0944386-16-4 $15.00

The Work of the Soul
Dr. Barbara Condron, ed. ISBN 0944386-17-2 $13.00

Uncommon Knowledge   Past Life & Health Readings
Dr. Barbara Condron, ed.   ISBN 0944386-19-9 $13.00

The Universal Language of Mind
The Book of Matthew Interpreted
Dr. Daniel R. Condron   ISBN 0944386-15-6 $13.00

Permanent Healing
Dr. Daniel R. Condron   ISBN 0944386-12-1 $9.95

Dreams of the Soul - The Yogi Sutras of Patanjali
Dr. Daniel R. Condron   ISBN 0944386-11-3 $13.00

Kundalini Rising
Mastering Your Creative Energies
Dr. Barbara Condron   ISBN 0944386-13-X $13.00

PeaceMaking
9 Lessons for Changing Yourself, Your Relationships and
Your World $13.00

To order write:

> School of Metaphysics
> World Headquarters
> 163 Moon Valley Road
> Windyville, Missouri 65783   U.S.A.

Enclose a check or money order payable in U.S. funds to SOM with any order. Please include $4.00 for postage and handling of books, $8 for international orders.

A complete catalogue of all book titles, audio lectures and courses, and videos is available upon request.

Visit us on the Internet at *http://www.som.org*
e-mail: som@som.org

We invite you to become a special part of our efforts to aid in enhancing and quickening the process of spiritual growth and mental evolution of the people of the world. The School of Metaphysics, a not-for-profit educational and service organization, has been in existence for three decades. During that time, we have taught tens of thousands directly through our course of study in applied metaphysics. We have elevated the awareness of millions through the many services we offer. If you would like to pursue the study of mind and the transformation of Self to a higher level of being and consciousness, you are invited to write to us at the School of Metaphysics World Headquarters in Windyville, Missouri 65783.

*The heart of the School of Metaphysic*s is a four-tiered course of study in understanding the mind in order to know the Self. Lessons introduce you to the Universal Laws and Truths which guide spiritual and physical evolution. Consciousness is explored and developed through mental and spiritual disciplines which enhance your physical life and enrich your soul progression. For every concept there is a means to employ it through developing your own potential. Level One includes concentration, visualization (focused imagery), meditation, and control of life force and creative energies, all foundations for exploring the multidimensional Self.

As experts in the Universal Language of Mind, we teach how to remember and understand the inner communication received through dreams. We are the sponsors of the National Dream Hotline®, an annual educational service offered the last weekend in April. Study centers are located throughout the Midwestern United States. If there is not a center near you, you can receive the first series of lessons through correspondence with a teacher at our headquarters.

For those desiring spiritual renewal, weekends at our Moon Valley Ranch on the College of Metaphysics campus in the Midwest U.S. offer calmness and clarity. Full Spectrum™ training is given during these Spiritual Focus Weekends. Each weekend focuses on intuitive research done specifically for you in your presence. More than a traditional class or seminar, these gatherings are experiences in multidimensional awareness of who you are, why you are here, where you came from, and where you are going.

The Universal Hour of Peace was initiated by the School of Metaphysics on October 24, 1995 in conjunction with the 50th anniversary of the United Nations. We believe that peace on earth is an idea whose time has come. To realize this dream, we invite you to join with others throughout the world by dedicating your thoughts and actions to peace for one hour beginning at 11:30 p.m. December 31st into the first day of January each year. Living peaceably begins by thinking peacefully. We invite SOMA members to convene Circles of Love in their cities during this hour. Please contact us about how you can become a Peace Correspondent.

There is the opportunity to aid in the growth and fulfillment of our work. Donations supporting the expansion of the School of Metaphysics' efforts are a valuable way for you to aid humanity. As a not-for-profit publishing house, SOM Publishing is dedicated to the continuing publication of research findings that promote peace, understanding and good will for all of Mankind. It is dependent upon the kindness and generosity of sponsors to do so. Authors donate their work and receive no royalties. We have many excellent manuscripts awaiting a benefactor.

One hundred percent of the donations made to the School of Metaphysics are used to expand our services. The world's first Peace Dome located on our college campus was funded entirely by individual contributions. Presently, donations are being received for the Octadome an international center for multidimensional living. Donations to the School of Metaphysics are tax-exempt under 501(c)(3) of the Internal Revenue Code. We appreciate your generosity. With the help of people like you, our dream of a place where anyone desiring Self awareness can receive education in mastering the mind, consciousness, and the Self will become a reality.

We send you our Circle of Love.

The Universal Peace Covenant

Peace is the breath of our spirit. It wells up from within the depths of our being to refresh, to heal, to inspire.

Peace is our birthright. Its eternal presence exists within us as a memory of where we have come from and as a vision of where we yearn to go.

Our world is in the midst of change. For millennia, we have contemplated, reasoned, and practiced the idea of peace. Yet the capacity to sustain peace eludes us. To transcend the limits of our own thinking we must acknowledge that peace is more than the cessation of conflict. For peace to move across the face of the earth we must realize, as the great philosophers and leaders before us, that all people desire peace. We hereby acknowledge this truth that is universal. Now humanity must desire those things that make for peace.

We affirm that peace is an idea whose time has come. We call upon humanity to stand united, responding to the need for peace. We call upon each individual to create and foster a personal vision for peace. We call upon each family to generate and nurture peace within the home. We call upon each nation to encourage and support peace among its citizens. We call upon each leader, be they in the private home, house of worship or place of labor, to be a living example of peace for only in this way can we expect peace to move across the face of the earth.

World Peace begins within ourselves. Arising from the spirit peace seeks expression through the mind, heart, and body of each individual. Government and laws cannot heal the heart. We must transcend whatever separates us. Through giving love and respect, dignity and comfort, we come to know peace. We learn to love our neighbors as we love ourselves bringing peace into the world. We hereby commit ourselves to this noble endeavor.

Peace is first a state of mind. Peace affords the greatest opportunity for growth and learning which leads to personal happiness. Self-direction promotes inner peace and therefore leads to outer peace. We vow to heal ourselves through forgiveness, gratitude, and prayer. We commit to causing each and every day to be a fulfillment of our potential, both human and divine.

Peace is active, the motion of silence, of faith, of accord, of service. It is not made in documents but in the minds and hearts of men and women. Peace is built through communication. The open exchange of ideas is necessary for discovery, for well-being, for growth, for progress whether within one person or among many. We vow to speak with sagacity, listen with equanimity, both free of prejudice, thus we will come to know that peace is liberty in tranquillity.

Peace is achieved by those who fulfill their part of a greater plan. Peace and security are attained by those societies where the individuals work closely to serve the common good of the whole. Peaceful coexistence between nations is the reflection of man's inner tranquillity magnified. Enlightened service to our fellowman brings peace to the one serving, and to the one receiving. We vow to live in peace by embracing truths that apply to us all.

Living peaceably begins by thinking peacefully. We stand on the threshold of peace-filled understanding. We come together, all of humanity, young and old of all cultures from all nations. We vow to stand together as citizens of the Earth knowing that every question has an answer, every issue a resolution. As we stand, united in common purpose, we hereby commit ourselves in thought and action so we might know the power of peace in our lifetimes.

Peace be with us all ways. May Peace Prevail On Earth.

created by teachers in the School of Metaphysics 1996-7